# Deprivation and Freedom

GW00789458

*Deprivation and Freedom* investigates the key issue of social deprivation. It develops a comprehensive yet refreshingly simple account of human freedom, which shows how the ability to realise one's freedom is partly definitive of freedom itself.

The subject matter of this book is vitally important and philosophically interesting, providing rigorous examination of a number of central themes and distinctions in ethical and political theory. These themes include Rawls' theory of justice, Nozick's libertarianism, acts and omissions, the doctrine of double effect, negative and positive rights, consequences, duties and of course freedom.

Richard Hull is already well-known for his work on disability and in this work has innovative things to say that connect disability with deprivation and freedom, illuminating all three concepts. Addressing crucial issues about deprivation, freedom, justice, democracy, and inclusion, this book will be of primary usefulness to students of moral, political and applied philosophy.

**Richard J. Hull** is Lecturer in Philosophy at the National University of Ireland, Galway.

# Routledge Studies in Ethics and Moral Theory

# Deprivation and Freedom

## A philosophical enquiry

**Richard J. Hull**

Routledge
Taylor & Francis Group

NEW YORK AND LONDON

First published 2007
by Routledge
270 Madison Avenue, New York, NY 10016

Simultaneously published in the UK
by Routledge
2 Park Square, Milton Park, Abingdon, Oxon OX14 4RN

*Routledge is an imprint of the Taylor & Francis Group, an informa business*

Transferred to Digital Printing 2009

© 2007 Richard J. Hull

Typeset in Times New Roman by Taylor & Francis Books

*Library of Congress Cataloging in Publication Data*
A catalogue record for the book has been request

*British Library Cataloguing in Publication Data*
A catalogue record for this book is available from the British Library

ISBN10: 0-415-37336-0 (hbk)
ISBN10: 0-415-80300-4 (pbk)
ISBN10: 0-203-94030-X (ebk)

ISBN13: 978-0-415-37336-4 (hbk)
ISBN13: 978-0-415-80300-7 (pbk)
ISBN13: 978-0-203-94030-3 (ebk)

**For my family**

# Contents

# Acknowledgements

I am very grateful to the supervisors of my graduate work at Oxford and Keele, much of which is represented here. Primarily, I am indebted to Jonathan Glover and Brian Smart for their incisive supervision and a generosity that has extended far beyond this project. I owe thanks to Jerry Cohen, who first made me think about the importance of the question of how serious it is to fail to provide in society. I was also very fortunate to be supervised on the work of Nietzsche by Bernard Williams, who was a source of great kindness, humour and acute advice. I cherish my conversations with him.

I am also very grateful to many people who have provided valuable comments and advice on all or parts of this work, although they are not at all to blame for it. They include John Baker, James Dwyer, Ricca Edmondson, Mark Haugaard, John Horton, David McNaughton, John Rogers, Tom Shakespeare, Hillel Steiner, Stephen Wilkinson and Jonathan Wolff.

An early version of Chapter 2 appeared in *Res Publica* ('Defining Disability: A Philosophical Approach', *Res Publica*, 1998, Vol. IV, 199–210), much of the material in Chapter 5 appeared in *Ethical Theory and Moral Practice* ('Deconstructing The Doctrine Of Double Effect', *Ethical Theory and Moral Practice*, 2000, Vol. 3, pp. 195–207) and assorted bits and pieces featured again in *Res Publica* ('Freedom: Not Flabby, Just Big Boned', *Res Publica*, 2000, Vol.6, 327–36). I would like to acknowledge the kind permission of Springer Science and Business Media to use that material here. I would also like to thank James Symonds for permission to print his superb and poignant photograph in Chapter 12.

Parts of this material have been delivered at the University of Manchester, University College Cork, University College Dublin, the World Congress of Bioethics in Brazil, the Medical College of Wisconsin and the University of Cape Town. I am grateful to all those who listened and who provided very useful comments. I am also grateful to very supportive colleagues and friends in the Department of Philosophy, NUI, Galway and to third-year and graduate philosophy students. Their questions and comments on lectures based on parts of this material have helped a great deal in my attempts to distil some of the themes that are developed here. In addition, I would like to thank Terry Clague and Katherine Carpenter at Routledge for their patience, advice and support, and Kate O'Brien for invaluable technical assistance toward the end of this project.

More generally, I would like to thank David Morrice and David Gosling who first encouraged me to believe that I could make some sort of contribution to this field. I would like to thank the Mellett family, who welcomed me to their beautiful and serene corner of the west coast of Ireland where this manuscript was completed, and Chloe for making the last months of this project much more enjoyable. Finally, I would like to thank my family, who give so very much more to me than they are likely to know. This book is dedicated to them with love, along with special affection and admiration for my brother Mark.

# Introduction

The subject of this book is human deprivation. Many people in society are deprived of the sorts of things that the majority of us take for granted. Indeed, many people are profoundly disadvantaged. This should be of concern to both the moral and the political theorist. This book examines the nature and gravity of different types of deprivation. It investigates the coherence of fairly modest claims with regard to social provision and enquires as to why, if these claims are coherent, society continues to do so very little about them.

Chapter 1, Relative social deprivation, investigates a variety of cases where people are disadvantaged in society. Those disadvantages are articulated as relative social deprivations. Different levels of deprivation are described with the hope that any reader will agree that, at the very least, we should be concerned with the most severe cases of social deprivation. The corresponding hope is that a readership as ideologically broad as possible will be motivated to read on. The deprivations described are then shown to be both social in nature and remediable. It is contended that the fact that much deprivation is a consequence of social structure is a widely agreed to sufficient condition to make it an issue of social justice. Indeed, a wide variety of theoretical perspectives converge on the judgement that it is important to question the justice of any social structures and practices that give rise to deprivations such as those described.

Chapter 2, Disability as social deprivation, looks at the specific case of disability in society as an example of deprivation. It is concerned with how disability should be defined. An accurate definition is crucial to our understanding of disability. It is established that disability can be secured either by functional limitation or by social discrimination and a new definition of disability reflecting this is introduced. In turn, a resolution to a long-standing conflict between the medical and social models of disability is presented. It is argued that the fact that disability can be socially induced presents it as an issue of social justice. Indeed, the discussion of disability in Chapter 2 provides a good test case for political and ethical theories and assists both our articulation and our comprehension of the kinds and severities of deprivations endured in more general cases.

Chapter 3, Deprivation as a restriction of freedom, presents deprivation as an issue of human freedom. While relative social deprivation and socially induced disability are very similar in nature, they are treated separately so to be both thorough and sensitive to the distinct experiences and challenges that can be bound up with different sorts of deprivation. Here, the distinction between freedom and ability is explored. The arguments of John Rawls, that natural primary goods should not be fully included in the equation of justice and that a person's inability only affects the worth of their liberty, are lengthily addressed. They are shown to have significant shortcomings. It is argued that one cannot be said in any meaningful sense to be free to do that which one is unable to do. A crucial distinction is made between legal or hypothetical freedom and realisable freedom. Realisable freedom is shown to be conditional upon ability. Then, using the characterisation of human freedom provided by Gerald MacCallum, the central claim is established that both relative social deprivation and socially induced disability are tantamount to unfreedom. Moreover, the kinds of freedom in question are shown to be important basic freedoms upon which the exercise of other freedoms is conditional. Given this, the question presents itself as to why such serious and remediable deprivations of freedom persist. An answer to that question is shown to revolve around the fact that society would have to make all sorts of provisions in order to secure freedom for those who are disabled and deprived. That fact supplies the theoretician with a variety of methods of evading responsibility for continued unfreedom.

Part Two of the book, Methods of evasion, investigates the coherence of different methods of evading responsibility for continued unfreedom in the cases of relative social deprivation and socially induced disability. It evaluates just how serious it is to fail to provide. The term 'social exclusion', while fashionable, is easily taken to imply that society is deliberately setting out to exclude people, which is an unfair assumption in many cases. It might be permissible to say that social practices are *exclusionary,* in that they have the effect of excluding, but to assert that the effect of excluding is the deliberate result of human *action* could be said to be philosophically evasive. Indeed, it is pertinent to the issue of social deprivation that we acknowledge that we are doing nothing or, at least, very little. Hence, the approach taken in this book is to investigate the moral seriousness of the weaker claim that society is merely failing to include. To show that 'mere failure', or non-inclusion, is morally reprehensible is a far more challenging line of inquiry and, if successful, provides a more accurate and robust critique of current social practices.

The idea, then, that the failure to provide is less morally serious than actively harming, that we are merely failing to include as opposed to socially excluding, is a potential justification for the continued failure to provide. That idea is scrutinised in Chapter 4, The doing/allowing distinction. It is argued that, although the conceptual distinction between harming and failing to help can be drawn, the claim that harming is *always* worse than failing to help cannot be established. It is shown that the failure to rectify a situation of harm cannot be excused solely by reference to its not being the result of positive agency. Likewise, the continuation of a situation of unfreedom cannot be justified solely by the claim that it has not been imposed. There are many more morally relevant factors requiring consideration.

Chapter 5, Knowledge and intention, considers the moral relevance of intention. Consideration of intention affects the moral evaluation of the failure to help. Moreover, denial of intention can itself amount to a method of evading responsibility for a given situation of harm. Attention is paid to the doctrine of double effect given that it makes a widely used distinction between intention and foresight and attaches moral significance to that distinction in the appraisal of harmful outcomes. It is argued that that distinction is often incorrectly drawn and that, when it is so drawn, the attaching of moral significance to it is evasive. What we can legitimately be said to intend is explored and it is contended that, if we know what the result of a given action or inaction will be, we must intend that it comes about if we go through with it. It follows from this that, if we have such knowledge, the denial of intention is not a legitimate means of evading responsibility for a given harmful outcome. (The ramifications of this with regard to the failure to provide in cases of relative social deprivation and socially induced disability are explored in Chapter 7.)

Attention is turned to other morally relevant factors that affect the overall moral status of a given course of conduct in Chapter 6, Consequences, duties and rights. The importance of consequence, preventability, commitments, duties and rights is established. They are seen to make a significant contribution to the moral evaluation of a given situation of harm irrespective of whether that harm is the result of positive or negative agency. It is therefore argued that, when evaluating the moral severity of the failure to provide in cases of relative social deprivation and socially induced disability, attention must be paid to those variables.

Chapter 7, Applications, investigates how the morally relevant factors described, along with consideration of intention, specifically apply to cases of relative social deprivation and socially induced disability. It is argued that all of those factors serve to contribute to the classifying of the failure to provide in these cases as morally reprehensible and that, indeed, there is a sense in which we can be said to intend that people continue to be deprived of important basic freedoms. Consideration of agency is shown to be outweighed by the application of other variables and it is argued, therefore, that recourse to the distinction between positive and negative agency is not a legitimate method of evading responsibility for the provision of important basic freedoms. Non-inclusion cannot be justified on the basis that it is *merely* non-inclusion. Rather, we should be obligated to provide with respect to relative social deprivation and socially induced disability.

Chapter 8, Nozick's retort, scrutinizes an alternative way of evading responsibility with regard to the provision of conditional basic freedoms. If we could be said to be entitled to *whatever* flows from the exercise of our natural assets, we could not be said to be obligated to provide for others. Robert Nozick argues that indeed we are entitled to whatever flows from the exercise of our natural assets. Weaknesses in his argument are identified. It is contended that the compelling reasons to provide in cases of relative social deprivation and socially induced disability recommend that we should not be entitled to all holdings that flow from the exercise of our natural assets. It is also shown that Nozick's theory fails to sufficiently acknowledge both the conceptual difficulty involved with defining a natural asset and the questionable nature of the relations between natural assets and social dis/advantages. From this it is concluded that Nozick's theory is an incomplete and unacceptable method of evading responsibility for important social provision.

Chapter 9, An argument from democracy, completes Part Two of the book by showing how the arguments hitherto presented cohere with the commonly accepted ideal of democracy. It is argued that, if we believe in the value of democracy, it is inconsistent to remain unsympathetic to those arguments. It is shown that the justification of democracy lies in the ideal of self-government tethered to the ideal of equality of respect for persons. From this it is argued that the endorsing of such ideals entails that we be obligated to provide in cases of relative social deprivation and socially induced disability. In as much as we value and respect other people, provision in these cases should be a matter of some urgency.

Given the considerable and remediable inequality of human freedom that has been identified, the compelling nature of the arguments recommending social provision and the failure of the methods of evasion discussed, Part Three of the book, Augmenting Reason, looks at ways of ensuring that we *actually do something about* relative social deprivation and socially induced disability. It attends to the idea that giving many a reason as to why we should provide might not necessarily motivate us to provide. It is contended that the use of other sources of understanding can both augment philosophical theory and motivate action so to alleviate the hardship of others.

Chapters 10 and 11 explore the rich resources provided by the work of Nietzsche, illustrating how the often perceived divide between analytic and continental philosophy both can and should be bridged. Chapter 10, Nietzsche's thought experiment, shows how the idea of eternal recurrence offers an alternative way of appreciating the subject at hand. It makes the conditions of the world in which we live intrinsic to the evaluation of our own lives. In this way, the plight of others is made more immediate to us. It is argued that, in so far as the idea of eternal recurrence makes considerations of justice more personal and urgent, attention to it augments the reasons as to why we should provide in cases of relative social deprivation and socially induced disability.

Chapter 11, The role of genealogy, provides more substance and colour to the subject at hand, namely, the hardships of other people. It is argued that the imaginative historical and psychological insights contained within

Nietzsche's *On the Genealogy of Morals* enrich our understanding of human hardship and that they can be both credibly and usefully incorporated into an analytic approach. Indeed, in arresting us to the uniqueness and complexity of people's distress, it is contended that Nietzsche's genealogy can, crucially, *motivate us* to do something about the deprivation of conditional basic freedoms. A Nietzschean genealogy is thus shown to be a valuable asset both to this enquiry and to philosophical enquiry more generally.

Finally, Chapter 12, Other ways of seeing, looks at further methods of motivating change. It is argued that, like Nietzsche's genealogy, literature and photography can further sensitise us to the gravity of the deprivations of human freedom being discussed and thereby motivate us to rectify them. Different motivational tactics are explored and, while they are shown to be more successful than moral theory with regard to effecting social change, it is argued that their use needs a sound theoretical basis. Having explored the pitfalls of appealing to sentiment, it is contended that, in so far as analytic philosophers are interested in motivating people to change the way that they treat others, they have good reason to employ alternative sources so to give their arguments more motivational force. Given that there are compelling arguments in favour of provision in cases of relative social deprivation and socially induced disability, the rest of the chapter presents some alternative sources in an attempt to motivate us to make that provision.

The alternative sources contained within Chapter 12 creatively, visually and literally document what amount to current realities faced by many people who find themselves deprived in one way or another. It is hoped that the theory presented in Parts One and Two of this book, supplemented by the other sources of understanding investigated in Part Three, might go some way to encourage us not to allow those realities to endure.

# Part One
# Deprivation and freedom

# 1 Relative social deprivation

This book is about deprivation, in many forms and with complex causes. In the next chapter, we will look at the more specific case of the deprivations faced in society by people with impairments. However, prior to that the more general case will be explored, that people without impairments can find themselves socially, economically and professionally isolated to a large extent. Rather than using the contentious word 'poverty' I am going to describe what can be claimed to be relative deprivations. Different severities of deprivation will be described with the presumption that, at the very least, we will agree that people are deprived in the most severe cases. That the deprivations discussed are, in the main, both social in nature and remediable will also be established and it will be argued that we really ought to worry a lot about the continuation of such deprivations in society.

Many people who live in what we consider to be advanced industrial societies could be described as poor. However, what should and should not count as poverty is a rather contentious issue. Thus, taking the UK as a case study and before looking at the limitations of ability and opportunities that are faced by many people, we must investigate just how they can be legitimately described. While calling them instances of poverty might be contestable, describing them as relative deprivations is more accurate and uncontentious. This has a bit to do with the so-called paradox of relative poverty, which will also be addressed.

The term poverty is commonly used in two ways. It is used to describe a state of affairs in an absolute sense or to describe a state of affairs relative to another. When one is described as poor in the absolute sense, one is said to be living at or below the level of subsistence.[1] The emphasis here is on biophysical survival: if one is poor, one's needs that make living possible are not met.[2]

> absolute poverty is seen as including a nutritionally inadequate diet, and not one inadequate in terms of some socially approved standard that may be influenced by fashion and culture. Rather a poverty-stricken diet is one inadequate to sustain life, or sustains life only, leaving little in reserve for work, never mind the positive enjoyment of

life. Clothing and shelter are also necessities for the maintenance of life . . . Our biological nature requires warmth; therefore, fuel supplies are an additional necessity for life.[3]

The idea is, then, that we can define a minimum standard of living based on a person's needs for food, water, clothing and shelter and, if we live below it, we can legitimately be said to be poor.[4] It should be noted that this conception of poverty cannot be as absolute as it would like to be, for what it would cost to sustain life in the UK would obviously be more than in a developing world country, given the disparity in food prices. One would hope that an absolute poverty theorist would not recommend that people in the UK should only be given the resources necessary to sustain life in the country with the lowest food prices. Some relativity must be conceded. Indeed, Oppenheim argues that an absolute minimum must itself be defined by what is socially acceptable.[5] In principle, our needs for survival could be met on the absolute model without providing, for example, modern sanitation or electricity. This would not seem to be acceptable in a modern advanced society, yet it must be acceptable to an absolute poverty theorist unless he or she concedes Oppenheim's point. Nevertheless, the absolute conception of poverty does describe an intuitively appealing baseline. We can be said to be poor only when we have inadequate means to survive. To cry poverty when we do have adequate means for survival is both to misuse the word and to demean the predicament of those who do not have such means.

If the absolute conception of poverty emphasises the needs for survival, the relative conception of poverty tends to emphasise the needs for living in a more substantive or qualitative sense. This is because it tends to pinpoint the gap, or gulf, between those who enjoy a high standard of living and those in the same society who do not, even if they cannot be said to be poor in an absolute sense. If they could be said to be poor in an absolute sense, it would seem superfluous, even if accurate, to invoke the concept of relative poverty. The concept, then, becomes meaningfully operative only after subsistence has been achieved. It is quality of life that is the currency of the relative poverty theorist rather than life itself.

The idea behind the concept of relative poverty is that comparisons with others help to define what is counted as unfortunate.[6] So, while I may have been content to have eaten a baked potato washed down with home-made carrot juice in my tent every evening without fail for the past twelve years when everybody else did the same, I may justly feel relatively unfortunate now that most others laugh at my tent as they scooter past with burgeoning shopping baskets en route to three square meals with fine wine in their sparkling maisonettes, when I have no such opportunity. Indeed, in comparison with others, my life is impoverished. Poverty exists, then, under this conception 'if people are denied access to what is generally regarded as a reasonable standard and quality of life in that society'.[7] So, now that society has moved on and has a 'sufficiently rich resource and capital base',[8] it would not be unreasonable for me to want out of my tent and to be speedily rehoused.

To define poverty as relative to the living standards prevailing in a society seems to make a lot of sense.[9] That is to say, while I may not be needy in terms of subsistence, it would be reasonable to feel impoverished if the lives of those around me were radically different and qualitatively superior. However, Shaw argues that to entertain the concept of relative poverty is to entertain a paradox. Her example runs as follows:

> Society A is poorer than society B. In A subsistence may be taken for granted as the poverty line, yet many people or perhaps the majority may be for most of their lives just somewhat above it. In contrast in society B there is more wealth and no one is living below the subsistence line or even on it, at least judged by international standards. Yet in society B many people may come to believe they are poor if they cannot match up to a socially approved standard of living. Thus we arrive at the paradox that wealthy societies are more poverty-stricken than poor societies.'[10]

Although at first sight this may seem to be a paradox, it need be nothing of the sort. It would be paradoxical (in more than one sense) if, in accepting the idea of relative poverty, we rejected that of absolute poverty. This, however, is far from inevitable. Granted, there may well be more relative poverty in wealthy societies than in poor societies, but to stop there would be to neglect the fact that people in poor societies are absolutely poor or very close to it. If we run the two conceptions of poverty together, with the proviso that the moral claim of the absolute poor must take precedence over that of the relative poor,[11] then it is not true that 'wealthy societies are more poverty-stricken than poor societies'. That claim can only hold if either we adopt a conception of relative poverty at the expense of a conception of absolute poverty, or we forget the moral claim of the absolute poor as soon as they creep 'just somewhat above' the subsistence line. The former is unnecessary and the latter contradicts any concern for the subject at hand, namely, the hardship of others around us.[12] So, we need not be troubled by Shaw's somewhat creative accounting of the concept of poverty.

Both of the concepts described above articulate important intuitions with regard to different sources of human hardship. Moreover, they need not be mutually exclusive. Rather obviously, it is perfectly consistent to run the two concepts together. We can concede that, given the greater severity of hardship, the claims of the absolutely poor should outweigh the claims of the relatively poor. However, this is not to deny that relative poverty exists and, while its alleviation is less urgent than the alleviation of starvation and death, it is urgent nonetheless. Indeed, if we were unconcerned with what quality of life human beings can and should enjoy, saving life itself would seem to lose much of its motivation.

Although I have argued that it is not paradoxical to use the term relative poverty, in what follows I would like to leave room to describe instances of hardship where it could be seen to be inaccurate or a little excessive to describe them as instances of poverty. In the interests of not making the concept of poverty too elastic, such instances will be described as relative deprivations.[13] To describe a situation as one of relative deprivation both avoids the perceived contentiousness of invoking the term poverty and allows for situations where one could not be said to be poor but could be said to be deprived. Henceforth, we will see the ways in which and the degrees to which people in the UK could be said to be relatively deprived.

## Setting some levels[14]

If the level at which we should be unconcerned with deprivation were to be set at physical subsistence, one need not read on – 'For judged by the notion of absolute poverty there are no or few people in poverty in Britain.'[15] However, hardship of a considerable magnitude does exist in the UK and, while it is rarely on a par with absolute poverty, it is hardship nonetheless. This is especially accentuated given the prosperity of modern society. We have a 'sufficiently rich resource and capital base' to eradicate a lot of deprivation. This in effect makes the following material contextual. In another society or another world, certain deprivations might not be seen as deprivations. The more ambitious we become with regard to classifying deprivation, the more prosperity must be about so as to generate that classification and to make doing something about it an option. It is obvious, then, that, if matters were otherwise, so might be what follows.[16] I do not see that this poses a theoretical problem. What I suggest that we should be concerned with does not supersede concern at absolute poverty. Nor might I be suggesting that we be so concerned if things were different. However, things are not different – and it is not very contentious to claim that the more affluence and prosperity is enjoyed by human beings, the less we should tolerate the following states of affairs.

### *Homelessness*

Nearly all of us take for granted the fact that we have enough to eat and will continue to have enough to eat. Many of us also take for granted the fact that we will have somewhere to eat; somewhere secure where we choose to be. Some sort of shelter is vital to survival. What sort of shelter that should be is open to negotiation. In what follows, some people will be defined as homeless who *do* have a roof over their heads. However, what we should bear in mind is that there is an enormous difference between having a roof over one's head and having a home and that those who have a home tend to see it as something that it would be indecent for them to be without.

Even if sleeping in a shop doorway could be described as having shelter, it would be in poor taste to describe it as having a roof over one's head. The agency Shelter estimated that in 1992, for example, 8,000 people were sleeping rough in Britain.[17] Indeed, 1991 census data suggests that there were 10,000 rough sleepers and squatters.[18] Moving up the scale of luxury, on census day in 1991 there were approximately 100,000 single people in hostels and 22,000 families living in hostels or bed and breakfast hotels. Furthermore, there were 110,000 concealed families (such as those having to live with parents), 50,000 would-be couples living apart and 140,000 sharing households. This is not an inconsiderable sum of people who, although they could be said to have a roof over their heads, could not be said to have a home to speak of. Data is obviously open to interpretation but, even if we were to take the most conservative figure (the number of households accepted as homeless by local authorities, which largely excludes single homeless people and misses many others) in 1991, 151,720 households were accepted as homeless by local authorities.[19] At the other end of the scale, Shelter estimated in 1992 that, in addition to the 'official homeless', approximately one-and-three-quarter-million people were homeless in Britain.

Whichever statistic we accept as an indicator, there is not one small enough here to extinguish our concern. Waldron[20] encourages that concern by pointing out that the only salvation for those sleeping rough is collective property.

The homeless are allowed to be – provided they are on the streets, in the parks, or under the bridges. Some of them are allowed to crowd together into publicly provided 'shelters' after dark (although these are dangerous places and there are not nearly enough shelters for all of them). But in the daytime and, for many of them, all through the night, wandering in public places is their only option. When all else is privately owned, the sidewalks are their salvation. They are allowed to be in our society only to the extent that our society is communist.[21]

Waldron goes on to argue that the increasing regulation of public places, the formalisation of the distaste we feel when seeing homeless people, is 'one of the most callous and tyrannical exercises of power in modern times by a (comparatively) rich and complacent majority against a minority of their less fortunate human beings'.[22] That society has a choice in this matter is abundantly clear. Homelessness in a wealthy society is the offspring of that particular social set up. It simply need not follow from a condition of prosperity that people go without a roof over their heads. Likewise, it is not inevitable that families be cramped together in bed and breakfast hotels that do not meet minimum local authority standards and where it is often impossible to lead a normal family life.[23]

There can be no doubt, then, that being without shelter, being without a roof over one's head and being without any semblance of a home constitute severe disadvantages. Indeed, having a home is a precondition for all other aspects of life.[24] The security that it affords is essential for health, access to services and employment[25] and the ability to take part in the life of the community on any level with others, let alone on an equal one. So, to the extent that we value our homes and the sorts of lifestyles they facilitate, we should be gravely concerned that many people are without a home and, as a result, are physically, socially and economically isolated. Furthermore, if we concede that people should be able to take part in the life of their community, at least on some level, the question arises as to what we think is an appropriate level below which no one should be allowed to fall.

### *Living below income support level/below 50 per cent of average income*

Homeless people aside (they are ignored in the following statistics), there are many other people in the UK who could be said to be deprived. One way of measuring that deprivation is in terms of income. People with very low incomes go without lots of commodities and cannot explore opportunities that many of us take for granted. That they are relatively deprived will become clear in what follows.

Income support is set by the government and defines a level of income below which people could not be reasonably expected to live. If we think of what we earn and calculate the lowest income that we could foreseeably live on, we might be surprised to learn that in 1989, for example, the government set the minimum level of income at £33.40 per week for a single person over twenty-five, £51.45 for a couple and £79.10 for a couple with two children (after housing costs).[26] We might be further surprised to learn that in 1989, 4,350,000 people (8 per cent of the population) were living *below* that set minimum.[27] It is obvious here that the government need not set the minimum level of income so pitifully low and that it need not let people fall below that level. That is, the role of society in maintaining and perhaps intensifying deprivation cannot be denied in this case.

A slightly more courageous level, living below which one could be said to be relatively socially deprived, is that set by the 'Households below average income' statistics. Here, living below 50 per cent of average income is said to define unacceptable deprivation. That level is 'widely used by commentators and in international studies'.[28] It is slightly higher than the income support level. For example, in 1989, 50 per cent of average income was £46 per week for a single person, £83 for a couple and £115 for a couple with two children (after housing costs). However, these figures are still modest estimates of adequate living requirements and we must remember that they only constituted half of the average income in the UK at that time. Many might find the average itself rather unpalatable. That said, in 1989, 12 million people (22 per cent of the population) were living on an income below half of the average after housing costs (10.4 million were living below half of average income before housing costs).[29] In 1993/94, 13.7 million people (24 per cent of the population) were living on an income below half of the average after housing costs (10.7 million were living below half of average income before housing costs).[30] This is not an inconsiderable sum of people and the fact that they live on an income *below half of the average* amounts to a clear indication that they are relatively deprived.

It is not utopian, nor economically inconceivable, nor particularly impressive to assert that no one should be allowed to fall below an income that is half of the average in a society such as the UK, let alone below income support level. Indeed, we might go further. The following level below which we might agree that no one should be able to fall is hardly outrageous. It will also serve to underline the extent to which the people living at the levels hitherto discussed are relatively deprived.

### The breadline Britain survey and the modest but adequate budget

Another way of defining unacceptable deprivation is by compiling a list of necessities and seeing how many people go without them. Mack and Lansley[31] used public opinion surveys to find what people thought were necessities for a minimum standard of living. Having done that, they found in 1990 that approximately eleven million people went without three or more of those necessities. The necessities were articulated as follows:

- self-contained damp-free accommodation with an indoor toilet and bath;
- three daily meals for each child and two for adults;
- adequate bedrooms and beds;
- heating and carpeting;
- refrigerator and washing machine;
- enough money for special occasions like Christmas;
- toys for the children.[32]

If we take three or more of these necessities away, we are not left with much. It cannot be denied that we would be relatively deprived to a significant degree. In the interests of not being deprived to such a significant degree, it has been proposed that an appropriate level below which no one should be allowed to fall is defined by what is called a modest but adequate budget.

The modest but adequate budget provides both for items that are regarded as necessities in public opinion surveys and for items that more than half the population have. The emphasis here is on what people require to be able to take part in the life of the community as opposed to what they require to barely survive in it. That said, the budgeted items hardly smack of opulence. For example, one week's annual holiday is budgeted for but a holiday abroad is not. Basic cosmetics are included but not perfume. Taking children to a pantomime once every two years is budgeted for yet music lessons are not on the list.[33] When broken down into weekly financial requirements, in 1993 the modest but adequate budget amounted to £121.80 for a single man, £181.28 for a couple and £278.38 for a couple with two children (after housing costs). While this goes beyond the level at which we could reasonably be expected to survive in society, it does not go very far. It merely includes some of the things (and in their cheapest guise) that many of us take for granted in everyday life. It is also worth noting that the income support and half of average income levels go nowhere near providing for the sort of things taken into account by the modest but adequate budget. That is to say, in 1993 income support amounted to approximately 37 per cent of the modest but adequate budget, and the half of average income level amounted to approximately 48 per cent.[34]

The income support level and the half of average income level, then, amount to less than half of what was considered to be a modest but adequate budget for living in the UK at that time. This is not to forget the millions depicted earlier that live below even those levels. To deny that people living like this are relatively socially deprived to a significant degree would be to ignore a significant amount of (conservative) statistical evidence.

### *Other considerations*

It is difficult to put a price on some things, the lack of which could be said to contribute to relative deprivation. We have a concern for a certain level of economic well-being in so far as it facilitates experience that cannot be measured in fiscal terms. Along these lines, Goodin writes about the importance of non-material vulnerabilities, as does Jones. Jones argues that

> there is no reason to limit a common characterization of poverty as 'lacking the basic necessities of life' merely to those necessities that are bound up with material conditions that relate to biophysical survival. Nor is there any a priori reason to assume that only economic factors constitute the impoverishing causes of such conditions.[35]

While we all have needs for food and shelter, then, we also have psychological needs, for example for friendship and love. These kinds of things enable us to 'fashion a meaning and significance to our lives which provide us with a measure of wholeness, purpose and integrity'.[36] The inseparability of income and value of life cannot be denied here. Income on its own would mean very little to us if it did not facilitate activity that bestowed value on our lives. However, centring in on income statistics can ignore certain factors that, while they may be bound up with financial considerations, can contribute to a sense of deprivation irrespective of income levels. Any discussion of deprivation should thereby take such factors into account.

We have already come across friendship and love. One could feasibly be financially comfortable yet feel relatively socially deprived if one had no respect and was unloved in one's community. Whatever detracts from our sense of well-being (even if it is through no fault but our own) is relevant to a discussion of deprivation. Now while feeling relatively deprived in the above example may command no response by society, there are similar deprivations where money does not constitute the whole solution and where society can do something about them. We will briefly consider two examples; stigmatisation and aesthetic degradation.

Our need for love, care and friendship denotes the importance of other people to our lives. Being respected by others is an essential ingredient of our well-being, or our 'search for significance'. Jones asserts that 'stigmatization, which reifies people as inherently and hopelessly defective, radically undermines this search'.[37] He argues that people can be stigmatised who are not economically poor and that groups within society can be reduced to economic poverty or other forms of impoverishing deprivation through 'the marginalisation and stratification which such stigmatisation produces'.[38] It is obvious from this that, for certain groups in society, an improvement in income would at best only solve part of the problem and that, if we are genuinely concerned with their deprivation, we should be concerned with tackling the misguided social attitudes that serve to contribute to (or define) that deprivation.

Likewise, the contribution of aesthetics to our sense of well-being should not be denied. We might have sufficient income to facilitate activity of value, but to incessantly return to an insecure, unkempt and uniformly dull living environment cannot but detract from our psychological well-being. We could well be said, then, to be relatively socially deprived given the state of the environment in which we have little choice but to live. Further, that this is a social and remediable disadvantage cannot be denied.[39] I am not suggesting that we should all wake up in a chocolate box cottage by the sea on a sunny day, but merely that, in deciphering an appropriate level below which no one should be allowed to fall, we should attend to the impact of aesthetically offensive and downtreading environments. Spending may need to be imputed with aesthetic consideration.

## Which level?

So far, it has been shown that many people in the UK are relatively socially deprived to differing degrees and in various ways. It has also been shown that such deprivations are social in nature and remediable. The disadvantages charted are the offspring of and dependent upon a particular social set up. Even if we asserted that the appropriate level below which no one should fall should be that of having a roof over one's head, that still gives us a lot of people to worry about and a lot of thinking to do about how we structure our society. However, given the high level of affluence and prosperity in our society, it is further unclear as to why we tolerate people living on minuscule incomes in miserable environments. Indeed, we should seriously reflect on the experiences of deprivation endured by such people. We should also look at the ways in which we categorise people and the effects that those categorisations have. If we do this, we might agree that the appropriate level in our society below which no one should be allowed to fall is significantly higher than that of income support and that more than fiscal injection is required. Even if we do not want to go this far, there is ample cause to read on.

It might be objected here that relative deprivation is not a matter of social justice, that society is not integral to the experience of deprivation. Rather, it might be argued that deprivation is the result of the stupidity, ineptitude and worthlessness of those who are deprived. This objection is only relevant to, and lays the blame for relative deprivation firmly in, the private sphere (see note 39). With regard to such an objection, it is worth remembering Jones's earlier points about stigmatisation. Also, as will be seen in Chapter 2, it is dangerous to place the problem 'in' the people.[40] Jones argues that we would be wrong to point, for example, to the ineptitude or apathy of people as responsible for generating deprivation. Rather, if people are apathetic, they are apathetic 'in the face of a substantive lack of opportunities or means to act. Such apathy clearly must be understood with reference to the social factors that produce it'.[41] We should be thinking, then, about the impact of cycles of deprivation over time rather than hastily absolving ourselves via misdirected blame.

Moreover, even if we conceded that people were in part to blame in some cases where they found themselves relatively deprived, 'to suggest that others should (or even that they may) stand idly by and watch people reap the bitter fruits of their own improvidence, is surely absurd'.[42] People who are relatively deprived are enormously vulnerable whether it is their fault or not and, on Goodin's analysis, such vulnerabilities generate strong responsibilities.

The point is, then, that people who are relatively socially deprived need not be so deprived. The deprivations described above are overwhelmingly attributable to a particular social set up both for their generation and continuation. Thus, whichever level we deem appropriate (and I have suggested that we ought to aim high), the social nature of the corresponding deprivations demands that they be seen as raising serious issues of social justice. In the next chapter, it will be shown that many of these considerations are also pertinent when thinking about the experience of disability in society.

# 2 Disability as social deprivation

This chapter will discuss the practical manifestations of disability in society as a specific example of social deprivation. We will come to see that the issue of disability provides a good test case for political and ethical theories. It introduces further considerations and complexities that any theory of just distribution would do well to address. It also develops both our articulation and comprehension of the kinds and severities of deprivation described in Chapter 1. Here it will be shown that much disability is primarily social and remediable. Any definition of disability ought to take this into account. The definition of disability that we will arrive at shows that disability is an issue of social justice, one that political and ethical theories should no longer neglect.

Political theory assumes and evolves around a picture of the human being as 'able bodied'. Yet 14 per cent of the adult population of the UK have disabilities. Disabled people in the UK are severely disadvantaged and, in this chapter, the different sorts of disadvantages endured by disabled people will be described. It is only through eliciting the nature of the disadvantages that are bound up with the experience of disability that we may come to understand what disability is and adequately define it. It will be shown that people with disabilities suffer social disadvantages of a remediable kind and that, in many cases, the social disadvantage is the primary constituent of the disability. The whole concept of disability, post analysis, will be shown to be quite different from the way in which it is ordinarily understood.

Although fashionable, it would be inaccurate and evasive to deny that the 'material reality' of functional limitation has at least something to do with disabled people's experience of disadvantage. As Morris points out, the reality is that disabled people are often physically different from what is considered to be the norm:

> Our bodies generally look and behave differently from most other people's (even if we have an invisible physical disability there is usually something about the way our bodies behave that gives our difference away). It is not normal to have difficulty walking or to be unable to walk; it is not normal to be unable to see, to hear; it is not normal to be

incontinent, to have fits, to experience extreme tiredness, to be in constant pain; it is not normal to have a limb or limbs missing. If we have a learning disability the way we interact with others usually reveals our difference.'[1]

Many disabled people, then, experience some of these differences, not that the list is complete. And while it is important to acknowledge that a particular social context can help to define what we count as normal, such physical and psychological realities of functional limitation can serve to put disabled people at a disadvantage in everyday life. The experience of pain for example, while it should not be equated with disability, is disabling. Those who experience chronic pain simply are at a disadvantage if that experience precludes them from holding down a job, going shopping, eating out, enjoying a glorious view or doing anything important to their projects in life. While the example of chronic pain is admittedly extreme, I see no reason why 'chronic pain' could not be replaced with blindness, deafness, paralysis or other functional limitations, at least to go some way in explaining the experience of disadvantage. Adapting a point made by Söder,[2] we do not want functional limitations and do not tend to envy those who have them. In so far as the ability to act upon and satisfy our projects in life without hindrance is held to be valuable, the fact that functional limitation can be to some degree disadvantageous explains our lack of want and envy here.

So, the physical reality of functional limitation should not be overlooked in an explanation of disabled people's experience of disadvantage. This however is by no means the end of the story.

Disabled people face many challenges with regard to education, employment, health and social support services, housing, transport and the built environment, leisure, and social and political life. And some facts of the matter are important here if a theoretical approach is going to be sympathetic to the reality of the situation.

Mainstream education in the UK is largely segregated and inaccessible to disabled people. Disabled people only go to mainstream schools when they are seen not to pose problems to those schools. The resulting commonplace segregation in schooling for disabled children ensures that school leavers are 'socially immature and isolated'. With regard to higher education, disabled students find the majority of institutions inaccessible. Three per cent of disabled people under retirement age are studying in further education or adult training centres and disabled students constitute 0.3 per cent of the entire student population of Britain.[3] It is obvious here that mainstream education in the UK need not be segregative and inaccessible to disabled people. There is no inherent necessity, for example, to segregate disabled children from mainstream schools; this is a result of misguided or discriminatory attitudes, laws and environments. (Having said that, it is important to note that some children may benefit from some segregative schooling, for example those with serious hearing or speech difficulties).

Employment is also hard to obtain for disabled people in Britain. It is widely accepted that ...

> disabled people are more likely to be out of work than the rest of the community, they are out of work longer than other unemployed workers, and when they do find it, it is usually low paid, low status work with poor working conditions ... Assessment, rehabilitation and training rarely lead to mainstream employment, and the overwhelming majority of disabled workers in Government sponsored workshops are in low status occupations working for below subsistence wages.[4]

That disabled people are disproportionately disadvantaged with regard to employment prospects, in many cases has nothing to do with their functional limitation. Rather,

> institutional discrimination against disabled people is prevalent throughout the British labour market. Clearly, widespread prejudice and ignorance regarding disabled people's work potential persist among employers and able bodied workers. Moreover they are constantly being reinforced by a range of factors, both social and environmental, outside the context of the workplace which have a great effect in excluding disabled workers when they apply for work or seek promotion.[5]

The existence of welfare measures in the UK offers little consolation to the disproportionate number of unemployed people with disabilities. The additional costs of being disabled are grossly underestimated. The Office of Population, Censuses and Surveys estimated, for example, that disabled people's additional disability related costs were between £6.10 and £12 per week. However, the Disablement Income Group found at the very same time that additional costs relating to disability (for example, extra mobility, heating and clothing costs) amounted to between £49.86 and £86.73 per week.[6] That tends to indicate that welfare payments are insufficient to meet the extra costs entailed through being disabled; the basic allowance paid at that time to disabled people who had made no National Insurance contributions was £34.80 per week. It is highly implausible to contend here that the possession of a functional limitation necessarily entails that the Government seriously underestimates 'the true financial cost of impairment and the degree of economic deprivation suffered by most disabled people'. Rather, as was seen with relative social deprivation more generally, the role of society in upholding and contributing to disadvantage in this case is undeniable.

Types and experiences of disadvantage can again be seen to be dependent on a particular social set-up in the case of health and social support services. That is to say, it need not follow from one's being functionally limited that health and social support services restrict one's opportunities for economic and social integration. Yet this is the case in the UK. Disabled people have little autonomy, choice or control over the provision of health and social support services. They often have little authority over just who it is that will enter their home. In turn, many disabled people cannot afford choice – they cannot afford to purchase support services on the open market and so are dependent on financially overstretched local authorities for the satisfaction of their care needs. Local authority provision is much criticised:

> In terms of funding, services for disabled people are accorded a low priority within the present health and social support system ... Technical aids and equipment supply is split between a number of agencies in a way that creates confusion for all concerned ... and ... There is no national comprehensive personal assistance service for those disabled people who need it ... most of this work is done by unpaid, informal helpers, namely family and friends.[7]

Perhaps the most obvious disadvantages facing people with disabilities are with regard to the physical environment. Only a small percentage of homes are accessible to disabled people, 'all modern transport systems are to varying degrees inaccessible to disabled people' and, in the unlikely event of them reaching their destination, they face a 'predominately inaccessible built environment'.[8] As a result, the performance of everyday tasks is made significantly more difficult. Once again, to deny the importance of society in upholding and exacerbating disadvantage here would be mistaken. Restrictions on mobility have further ramifications, especially when coupled with the employment and financial difficulties detailed above. All serve to impede choice and together can comprise insurmountable barriers to participation in leisure activities, the enjoyment of entertainment, and involvement in mainstream political activity[9] – run of the mill things that we tend to take utterly for granted.

There can be no doubt, then, that people with disabilities in the UK are severely disadvantaged. These disadvantages add up to the fact that many people are socially, economically and professionally isolated to a large extent. Moreover, the social nature of many disadvantages is obvious. That is to say, the possession of a functional limitation need not entail a segregated, unsupportive and inaccessible society. So, any definition of disability ought to take the limitations posed by society into account, for society is integral to many of the disadvantages that are bound up with the experience of disability.

Conventional views of disability, while acknowledging the social manifestation of many disadvantages, tend to assume that, since they would not arise in the absence of functional limitation, those disadvantages must originate in functional limitation. This lends support to the view that disabled people should be grateful for any charitable measures granted in their favour but it is too swift and simple an assumption to make.

Disadvantage, as it presents itself here, is the offspring of the interaction of people and society. Without society people's functional limitations would be different, as would society be without functionally limited people. In this sense, both society and functional limitation are necessary conditions for disadvantage. Contrary to the conventional view, however, functional limitation does not always secure or guarantee disadvantage. Consideration of specific examples will show that society can be equally to blame or more to blame in many cases and this will bring us further toward the construction of an accurate definition of disability.

Consider again the disadvantages relating to the physical environment. As noted earlier, many people with disabilities face a predominantly inaccessible built environment. This is especially true of those who rely on wheels for locomotion as opposed to legs. One reason for the built environment being so inaccessible to those who use wheels to navigate it is the prevalence of stairs. So, in this case the disadvantages entailed by an inaccessible built environment, detailed earlier, evolve from the incompatibility of stairs and wheels.

This begs the question as to what guarantees that one be disadvantaged in this case. Assuming that the physical reality of functional limitation guarantees disadvantage, we must ask whether the reliance on wheels for locomotion necessarily leads to disadvantage in this particular case. If it does not, then presumably the guarantor of the disadvantage in question, namely, reduced environmental access, cannot be functional limitation and we must think again. The fact that if ramps and lifts were more common than stairs, people who rely on wheels for locomotion would not be disadvantaged in their pursuit of the many and wide ranging activities that stairs prohibit, does indeed urge us to think again. That is to say, it does not follow from being functionally limited as to the use of one's legs, that one be necessarily disadvantaged in accessing the built environment. Functional limitation does not guarantee disadvantage here. Rather, exclusive architecture ensures the experience of disadvantage in this case. If architecture was more sympathetic to wheels, those who rely on wheels for locomotion would face no disadvantage in accessing the built environment and, by implication, would not be constrained by the many disadvantages that are the offspring of an inaccessible built environment. The only disadvantages that could be held to be secured solely by the functional limitation with regard to this example are those evolving from the pursuit of activities that depend solely on legs for their execution, for example the disadvantage of not being able to *walk* the Pennine Way, *climb* Everest or be an Olympic *sprinter*. Accessing the built environment need not entail, in all but a few cases, dependence on legs. Thus, it is a mistake to equate the disadvantage of being unable to gain access to the built environment with the functional limitation of not being able to walk. Exclusive architecture[10] is the element of the interaction between person and society that secures the disadvantage in this particular case.

This example serves to illustrate that any definition of disability must differentiate between functional limitation and society when accounting for disadvantage. We can point to what, within the said interaction between person and society, secures disadvantage in a particular case. This is not to deny that functional limitation is an important component in the interaction between person and society in the case of disability: the problem of environmental accessibility would not present itself here if people did not have certain functional limitations. The point is that the problem would not exist if architectural design took those functional limitations into account.

Consider a bizarre evolutionary twist: 86 per cent of the population develop springs on their feet with fantastic jumping capabilities – a common side effect, let's say, of eating too many genetically modified tomatoes. You and I form part of the 14 per cent of the population who lack springs. We could have failed to develop them, broken them or they might have lost their power due to old age or illness. The upshot is that we are now relatively hopeless at jumping and outnumbered by those who are not.

Bounding along (in so far as we can) to the opening of our favourite but newly rebuilt superstore one day, we are met with a shocking surprise. There are no stairs or lifts to the first floor. Our spring-footed peers find it quicker and less arduous to jump to the first floor. We are told that stairs are now an extravagance, a waste of resources, but reassured by the management that there will be a sample selection of merchandise on show for us on the ground floor. They acknowledge that this is not an ideal state of affairs for the springless, but they pledge to recruit more staff over the next five years who will be specifically trained to help us.

I do not imagine that we would think very highly of that particular architectural initiative, especially if the excellent jazz section was on the fourth floor of the building – and the bar was on the fifth. Of course, somebody could (eventually) bring merchandise down to the ground floor for us to look at (if we knew what we wanted) or we could order online, but it would not be the same as actually being able to negotiate the new store in its entirety. Indeed, the point here is that all we need be missing out on *by necessity*, given our lack of springs, is doing at all well in high jump competitions. Yet suddenly, in this example, our functional limitation has become a considerable disadvantage due to exclusive architecture. Society is effectively ignoring the 14 per cent of its population who lack springs. And, granted, the problem would not arise if we all had springs, but nor would it exist given more sympathetic building design.

Coming back down to earth, consider another example: if I am colour blind, institutional discrimination may prevent my getting a job as a silver service waitress, but my functional limitation will prevent me securing a job as a hair colourist, in all but the most adventurous of salons. The disadvantage, my joblessness, is the same in both cases yet what ensures that disadvantage is different: my functional limitation in the latter case but, in the former, a response to my functional limitation that is far from inevitable or fair.

Of course, things are rarely this simple in reality. Disadvantage more often than not involves a complex interplay of functional limitation and social factors. Nonetheless, when we are thinking about disability issues, it is useful to distinguish disadvantages that result primarily from functional limitation from those that result primarily from a socially inadequate response to that functional limitation. The examples serve to illustrate that. Moreover, they show that while exclusive architecture and institutional discrimination in the given cases have a subject, me, the resulting disadvantages need not follow from my functional limitation and, furthermore, would not exist given different social provision. And while there are admittedly differences with regard to intention and hostility, exclusive architecture and institutional discrimination in these cases exhibit similarities with racism and homophobia. It will be seen in what follows that these sorts of considerations are only partially evident in current definitions of disability.

Hitherto, I have tried wherever possible to avoid invoking the terms 'impairment' and 'disability' so as not to import any definitional bias prior to an elucidation of the concrete practical manifestations of disability. All that has been assumed so far is that the subject of discussion is disability (as a specific form of deprivation) and that people with disabilities are at all sorts of disadvantages detailed above. This does not assume agreement as to what disability is, just that people are as a matter of fact disabled. What has become evident from the investigation into particular disadvantages facing disabled people is that both the realities of functional limitation and social discrimination can secure disadvantage and thus that both need to be taken into account in any discussion of disability. Having become clear on this, we are now able to give content to the terms 'impairment' and 'disability'.

The easiest claim to make here is that functional limitation and impairment are one and the same thing. I have avoided using the term 'impairment' simply because it is used for the purpose of defining disability. This was perhaps overcautious, but safeguards against the accusation of adopting a model of disability prior to defining it. That aside, it is not a controversial claim to make that functional limitation implies impairment and vice versa. The difference between the two terms is merely syntactic.

The second claim supported by the arguments so far, is that disability and disadvantage (as employed in the above discussion) are one and the same thing. It has been shown that, in the context of this debate, one is disadvantaged because of the reality of impairment or because of the reality of social discrimination, or both. In the process of making these deductions, it was also shown that one need not be disadvantaged by a functional limitation except where a pursuit solely requires the use of that which one is functionally limited in using. If the further obvious assumption is made, that being disabled entails not being able to do something, then we cannot hold disability to be synonymous with functional limitation, for it would be absurd to claim that one is not disadvantaged by functional limitation, that is, not limited in pursuing a certain goal yet, at the same time, is disabled by functional limitation, in pursuing that very same goal. Thus, unless we deem it coherent to say that one can be able to do *x* and at the same time be disabled from doing *x*, then being able to do *x* is to not be disabled from doing *x* and being unable to do *x* is to be disabled from doing *x*; and since not being able to do something is a condition of disadvantage, there is an equivalence between disability and disadvantage.

Likewise, disability cannot be held to be synonymous with social inadequacy or discrimination since people are not always rendered unable to do certain things, and by implication disabled, by social discrimination alone. To assume such a position would be to effectively ignore a fundamental component of disability, namely, functional limitation. In the interests of not doing this, it is appropriate in the context of this discussion to equate disability with disadvantage.

Furthermore, we would be left wondering what the origins of disability could possibly be, if not the very same as the origins of disadvantage. It is highly plausible to contend that, as in the case of disadvantage, disability is the offspring of the interaction of people with functional limitations and society. It is hard to think of anything else from which disability could originate. So it is equally plausible to contend that disability is tantamount to disadvantage. It has been important, however, to leave the term 'disability' aside until now, for its earlier inclusion could have imported possibly erroneous definitional preconceptions that may in turn have precluded the eliciting of the origins of disadvantage. Through investigation, those origins have materialised as the origins of disability. If the interchangeability of the two terms is granted, validity is conferred upon the claim that people with functional limitations (or impairments) are at all sorts of disadvantages, that is, they are disabled and that the overriding contribution to that disability can be either impairment or social discrimination. This is not widely appreciated.

Definitions of disability typically fall into two camps, both ignoring one of the aspects of disability elicited above. The World Health Organisation definition has the 'widest official usage' and runs as follows:

- Impairment: any loss or abnormality of psychological, physiological or anatomical structure or function.
- Disability: any restriction or lack of ability (resulting from an impairment) to perform an activity in the manner or within the range considered normal for a human being.
- Handicap: a disadvantage for a given individual, resulting from an impairment or disability, that limits or prevents the fulfilment of a role (depending on age, sex and social and cultural factors) for that individual.[11]

The emphasis of this definition is on disability as a purely physical and unalterable 'personal tragedy'. All disadvantage (handicap) here is held to originate in functional limitation. 'It assumes that disability and handicap are caused by psychological or physiological abnormality or impairment, and therefore the impairment is the primary focus of attention.'[12] No attention is paid to the reality depicted earlier that some disability is secured by social inadequacy or discrimination. Therefore, this definition only tells half the story. To neglect the social aspect of much disability, in the language of Lukacs, is to suffer from a 'reified' view of disability, whereby disability is mistakenly viewed as being natural and fixed.

The second definition, while not suffering from a 'reified' view of disability, goes too far in the other direction. It is an articulation by Disabled People's International of what is called the 'social model' of disability and runs as follows:

- Impairment: the functional limitation within the individual caused by physical, mental or sensory impairment.
- Disability: the loss or limitation of opportunities to take part in the normal life of the community on an equal level with others due to physical or social barriers.[13]

Although this definition is widely accepted by disability organisations and activists, it is ambiguous with regard to what counts as a 'physical' barrier. It is unclear as to whether 'physical' refers to functional limitation or to environmental inaccessibility. In its favour, this definition picks up on the omission of the WHO definition: 'These definitions allow for people to have an impairment without having a disability. If society was arranged in such a way that the functional loss had no impact there would be no handicap or disability.'[14] However, while this is an important statement about the social component and the alterability of some disability, it could be held to neglect the reality of impairment which can and does cause disability.

Thus, both the WHO and DPI definitions have shortcomings. The WHO definition neglects the fact that social factors can make the primary contribution to some disablement and the DPI definition does not clearly articulate the fact that the physical reality of impairment can ensure some disablement. Although further difficulties could be mentioned, especially with the WHO definition, the problems already cited give us ample cause to move on. What has become evident throughout the discussion is that any definition of disability, if it is to accurately reflect the experience of disability, must pay homage to both the reality of impairment and the reality of social inadequacy and discrimination. The following is a working model of disability that reflects the discussion so far:

- Impairment: physical, mental or sensory functional limitation.
- Impairment-induced disability: the loss or limitation of ability or opportunities to take part in the life of the community on an equal level with others due to impairment.

- Socially induced disability: the loss or limitation of ability or opportunities for people with impairments to take part in the life of the community on an equal level with others due to economic, political, social, legal, environmental and interpersonal barriers or failures.

This definition articulates the intuitions about the nature of disability that have been derived from this chapter's investigation. It reconceptualises disability, but not at the expense of the physical reality of impairment. Furthermore, the emphasis on socially induced disability posits the issue of disability firmly in the arena of social justice, for the disadvantages so described are not located with or guaranteed by impairment, but are overwhelmingly attributable to a particular set of social structures and arrangements. This is of fundamental importance to political theory, since the issue has been neglected and an impoverished and reified concept of disability often deployed. Many have failed to acknowledge or sufficiently acknowledge that the fact that people with impairments cannot do many things in society can – and does – have very little to do with their impairment. When the issue is presented in this way, discussions limited to charity and welfare no longer provide an appropriate response. The social aspect of much disability demands that it be seen as an issue that raises serious concerns about social justice.

While not wishing to detract in any way whatsoever from the uniqueness of different people's experiences, the similarities between relative social deprivation and the social aspect of disability are obvious. At the very least, in both cases we have been looking at social disadvantages of a remediable kind. Moreover, we have seen that both the social aspect of disability and relative social deprivation more generally urge us to question the justice of our present social structures and arrangements. In the next chapter, I will suggest that a useful way of doing that is via a concept of human freedom.

# 3   Deprivation as a restriction of freedom

Having looked at the issues of disability and relative deprivation more generally, and seen that they raise serious concerns about the justice of our social structures and arrangements, this chapter will articulate those concerns as concerns about inequalities of human freedom. While we have seen that relative social deprivation and socially induced disability are very similar in nature, they are treated separately here so as to be both thorough and sensitive to the distinct experiences and challenges that can be bound up with different sorts of deprivation. Having said that, for brevity I will at times refer to deprivation in a way that is taken to include both the general case of relative social deprivation discussed in Chapter 1 and the more specific case of the social aspect of disability discussed in Chapter 2.

A position opposed to the one that will be developed here is provided by John Rawls. He argues both that natural primary goods should not be included as fully in the equation of justice as they might be and that our inability to do something does not affect our freedom to do it, only the worth of that freedom. Rawls' ideas will be explored and will be shown to have significant shortcomings. A distinction will then be introduced between legal or hypothetical freedom and realisable freedom. I will argue that realisable freedom is conditional upon ability. And, using the characterisation of human freedom provided by MacCallum, the central claim will be established that both relative social deprivation and socially induced disability are instances of unfreedom. That done, we can move on to an evaluation of the arguments supporting the continuation of what is a remediable state of unfreedom.

## Negative liberty

Discussions of liberty over the past thirty years have often concentrated upon the negative/positive distinction. An elucidation of the defects of various conceptions of negative and positive liberty or freedom (I will take the terms to be interchangeable) is not the central concern of this book. However, the idea of negative liberty demands some attention, since

—

the adoption of a negative conception of liberty is often the starting point in contemporary political theory. Rival theories often criticise one another from the same negative conceptual standpoint. I want to argue that this artificially limits the scope of unfreedom and thus the scope of political debate. As things are, people who are relatively deprived, including people with impairments, are unable to talk about the social disadvantages that they face in terms of freedom. That is not right or fair. It will also be shown that any political theory would do well to take into account the point that any kind of freedom has both positive and negative elements.

The absence of external constraints is the central condition of negative liberty. Hobbes wrote that 'Liberty, or freedome, signifieth (properly) the absence of Opposition; (by Opposition. I mean external Impediments of motion)'[1] and, as Miller notes, 'this has become the dominant view of liberty in practical politics and in the writing of many liberal theorists'.[2] Freedom here is seen as natural and given. Thus, the absence of interference by external agents is sufficient for its realisation. As long as you are left alone, you are free. In addition, negative liberty theorists tend to stipulate what counts as an external obstacle to freedom. For example, natural obstacles are said not to violate freedom: 'I am rendered unfree by an obstacle, only if that obstacle is imposed by another person, not if it is the result of an accident of nature.'[3] Likewise, it is held that obstacles have to be external to impede freedom. It can be argued from this sort of position that, for example, people with physical impairments face a natural and internal obstacle which, by definition, cannot impede freedom. A physical impairment 'reduces the agent's ability, but not her freedom'.[4]

It is the nature of the distinction between freedom and ability that is of interest here. The negative position allows that one can be free to do that which one is unable to do. So, for example, you could be said to be free to walk to the shops even though you happened to be stuck in an enormous snowdrift. Yet, through limiting what counts as unfreedom in this way, many more serious incapacities or deprivations are denied the moral severity that attaches to claims of unfreedom. Social injustices can therefore be hidden under the blanket claim that we are all (negatively) free. No matter what we may think of our society, at least we all have our freedom. And, while true in at least one important sense, this claim is evasive and it gives freedom a rather mysterious air.

To illustrate this point, let us suppose that I want to jump from a second floor balcony, perform a somersault and land without any pain or injury – I am anxious to relive my gymnastic youth. I am free to jump from the balcony – nobody will stop me – but I am not able to do so without inducing serious injury upon landing. I am not, nor was I ever, an acrobat. However, I am able to jump from the balcony and induce serious injury upon landing. That is rather easy. The question is, though, in what sense can I be said to be free to jump from the balcony *without* inducing serious injury upon landing? I could be said to be conceptually or legally free to jump from the balcony without suffering pain or injury on landing, but in reality this freedom means very little to me unless I am also able to physically make such a jump. We might justly ask, then, why a freedom that means almost nothing[5] to me is called a freedom, given the political and moral connotations of the word.

John Rawls' *A Theory of Justice* goes against the intuitively appealing idea advanced above, that one cannot in a meaningful sense be said to be free to do that which one is unable to do. Rawls does this both by taking inadequate account of natural primary goods (like health) in the equation of justice and by invoking the worth of liberty distinction. With respect to the subject at hand, this has three interesting ramifications: (1) The inequalities in people's abilities to take advantage of their social primary goods due to natural disadvantages are largely ignored. So, for example, the extra costs associated with physical impairment are not taken into account when considering how to distribute resources. (2) Inequalities in people's abilities to take advantage of their social primary goods due to natural disadvantages, like impairment, are said not to affect liberty. They are said not to restrict our freedom, even if they stop us from doing all sorts of things. (3) Inequalities in people's abilities to take advantage of their social primary goods due to unequal economic means do not count as inequalities in liberty. That is, money does not affect freedom. Correspondingly, it follows that both relative social deprivation and socially induced disability are not tantamount to unfreedom. However, to tell a homeless person that he or she is free to buy a house, or a person in a wheelchair at the bottom of a flight of stairs that he or she is free to climb them, seems to demean the concept of freedom. It reduces freedom to something thoroughly unimportant and meaningless to a lot of people. To the extent that we are uncomfortable with such a position, it is important to look more precisely at what Rawls is saying.

## Rawls and natural primary goods

Underpinning Rawls' theory of justice is the intuitive idea that morally arbitrary factors should not determine the value of people's life chances. The original position is a device designed to represent what we believe to be the essentials of the moral equality of persons. It follows for Rawls that, from this position, we will choose principles of justice that apply to morally equal people. However, in order that we do not exploit our morally arbitrary advantages or choose principles of justice that exclusively favour ourselves, Rawls insists that in the original position we place ourselves behind a veil of ignorance. The evolution of fair principles of justice requires this veil according to Rawls, behind which no one knows his place in society, his class position or social status, nor does anyone know his fortune in the distribution of natural assets and abilities, his intelligence, strength, and the like. I shall even assume that the parties do not know their conceptions of the good or their special psychological propensities ... This ensures that no one is advantaged or disadvantaged in the choice of principles by the outcome of natural chance or the contingency of social circumstances. Since all are similarly situated and no one is able to favour his particular condition, the principles of justice are the result of a fair agreement or bargain.[6]

Rawls further stipulates that, in the original position, agents are rational in the sense that they can identify preferences between options and can calculate the best means to the chosen options. Additionally, to be totally ignorant would render us unable to make any informed choices from the original position. So, Rawls takes for granted that we know the general facts about human society, that we understand political affairs and the principles of economic theory, and that we know the basis of social organisation and the laws of human psychology.[7] He also takes for granted that we have a 'thin' theory of the good, that agents 'know in general that they must try to protect their liberties, widen their opportunities, and enlarge their means for promoting their aims, whatever these are ... they assume that they would prefer more primary social goods rather than less'.[8]

It is from this original position, then, that Rawls thinks we will be able to decide upon principles of justice that are applicable to morally equal people. We will make an impartial and unanimous choice with regard to the correct distribution of social primary goods, those being the goods that enable us to 'frame, revise, and rationally to pursue' our own (more comprehensive) conception of the good.

What principle(s) of distribution will be generated by the original position? Rawls argues that we will choose our principles of justice (from behind the veil of ignorance in the original position) via the 'maximin' strategy. He contends that it is rational for those in the original position to maximise the minimum position. Since the choosers are behind the veil of ignorance, they do not know what their situation in society will be. The idea is, then, that we should maximise the minimum position through fear that it could be ours. That said, Rawls asserts that agents in the original position, concerned with enlarging the means for promoting their aims but ignorant of their natural endowments, would choose the following principles of justice:

First principle – Each person is to have an equal right to the most extensive total system of equal basic liberties compatible with a similar system of liberty for all.

Second principle – Social and economic inequalities are to be arranged so that they are both:

(a) to the greatest benefit of the least advantaged, consistent with the just savings principle, and

(b) attached to offices and positions open to all under conditions of fair equality of opportunity.

First Priority Rule (The Priority of Liberty) – The principles of justice are to be ranked in lexical order and therefore liberty can be restricted only for the sake of liberty. Second Priority Rule (The Priority of Justice over Efficiency and Welfare) – The second principle of justice is lexically prior to the principle of efficiency and to that of maximising the sum of advantages; and fair opportunity is prior to the difference principle.[9]

On the face of it, a commitment to an equal right to the most extensive total system of equal basic liberties would receive a warm welcome from those who are seriously relatively deprived or disabled to a large extent by the society in which they live. However, the meaning and magnitude of Rawls' first principle will be shown to be greatly diminished, if not rendered an almost empty gesture, by both his failure to take adequate account of natural primary goods and his adherence to the worth of liberty distinction.

Now it is worth pointing out here that there is an obvious sense in which Rawls *does* take account of natural primary goods. Indeed, concern about where the exploitation of our unequally distributed natural talents and abilities might leave many of us in an unregulated free market system could be said to be the main motivation for Rawls to devise his system of justice as fairness. The difference principle, for example, is all about compensating those with less natural talents and abilities or, at least, those who are less able to exercise them for one reason or another. It is with this obvious sense in mind that I would like to proceed. Yet, while Rawls' concern is more than honourable, problems arise for him because, when considering the justice of different distributive schemes, he defines the worst off in terms of the social primary goods that they possess. For him, our concern in the original position will be with the distribution of such goods. He writes:

> The primary social goods ... are rights and liberties, opportunities and powers, income and wealth ... They are social goods in view of their connection with the basic structure; liberties and powers are defined by the rules of major institutions and the distribution of income and wealth is regulated by them ... The fundamental liberties are always equal, and there is fair equality of opportunity ... the primary social goods that vary in their distribution are the powers and prerogatives of authority, and income and wealth.[10]

However, it is questionable as to whether, if we were concerned with the position of the worst off in society, we would simply choose a distribution of social primary goods from the original position *without* being concerned with the impact that natural disadvantage might have upon what we could make of such goods.

Barry asks whether it would be rational for those in the original position to agree on any principles defined in terms of social primary goods. He finds the implications of agreement on principles defined in terms of social primary goods astonishing, since justice as fairness does not look behind the use that persons can make of the rights and opportunities available to them.

> For Rawls a pound is a pound is a pound. Whether some people need more pounds to get to the same place as others is irrelevant. The result of this dogma is to prevent anyone from being able to claim that because of special handicaps or disadvantages he needs more income than other people to achieve the same satisfaction.[11]

Kymlicka similarly argues that Rawls is mistaken in not looking at people's possession of natural primary goods when determining who is worst off. He asserts that there are good reasons for recognising natural handicaps as 'grounds for compensation' and that we should thus include natural primary goods in the equation when generating principles of justice from the original position.

> The difference principle may ensure that I have the same bundle of social goods as a handicapped person. But the handicapped person faces extra medical and transportation costs. She faces an undeserved burden in her ability to lead a satisfactory life, a burden caused by her circumstances, not her choices. The difference principle allows, rather than removes, that burden.[12]

On this account, then, we would only choose Rawls' principles if we found it fitting to ignore claims based on special need.

Thomas Pogge describes Rawls' position here as semiconsequentialist.[13] He contrasts this with full consequentialism, 'which holds that a conception of justice must pay attention not only to the distribution of social goods but also to differences in persons' physical and mental constitutions'.[14] If we were full consequentialists, then, we would most likely want to compensate for natural differences where those differences lead to inequalities in people's abilities to take advantage of their social primary goods. Rawls has little to say with regard to this possibility[15] and what he does say, as Pogge points out, sidesteps the issue:

> these remarks address only the easier cases, bypassing the difficult question of how to cope with those manifest and objective interpersonal differences in needs for and capacities to take advantage of social primary goods for which persons are not themselves responsible

and to which they can adjust themselves only with great difficulty, if at all. The serious problem for Rawls is the contention that for purposes of identifying the worst position, special gifts and natural handicaps (special disabilities or needs) should be taken into account.[16]

Nevertheless, Pogge argues that Rawls' semiconsequentialism comprises a 'plausible intermediate point' whereby 'justification is required insofar as institutions generate unequal incomes for persons working equally hard; the disadvantaged are those with the lowest incomes, regardless of their specific natural capabilities or needs'.[17] This is contrasted with the idea of defining positions in terms of income *and* natural attributes, 'in which case equality of income for persons working equally hard would require special justification because it would disadvantage the naturally handicapped vis-à-vis the naturally gifted'.[18]

Rawls' semiconsequentialism might well be plausible, but we can question whether, given the objections cited by Barry and Kymlicka above, it is acceptable. Pogge defends Rawls' semiconsequentialism by attacking the idea of including natural primary goods more fully in the equation of justice. He draws attention to the question of where we can legitimately draw the line in our assessment of plausible candidates for compensation when including natural primary goods. That is to say, it is not obvious to Pogge which natural disadvantages, if not all, should be taken into account and why.

When discussing medical care, Pogge argues that, if we were to take account of natural primary goods (when measuring distributive shares for purposes of assessing the justice of social institutions) in the case of medical needs, it would then be hard to legitimately rule out taking account of natural primary goods in other areas.

> If we take differences in persons' native medical needs into account in interpersonal comparisons, then why shouldn't we have regard to other congenital differences too? Once the original position is redescribed so that the parties care not merely about social positions (representative shares) but also about medical needs, then why would they not be concerned with the worst overall situation? Why would they not, in assessing the distribution of income, bear in mind that appealing clothes are more important for the ugly or instruments for those especially musical? Why wouldn't they, in assessing the distribution of education, also take account of the fact that some learn more slowly and thus need more education to acquire the same knowledge or skills?[19]

It may indeed be difficult, then, to rule out taking account of natural primary goods in other areas once we consider them in the case of medical needs. However, it is not obvious that this constitutes a problem for what Pogge calls the fully consequentialist approach. It can be argued that we should take account of natural differences *in any area* where those differences have profoundly detrimental effects. So, with regard to Kymlicka's example, we should compensate for a disabled person's extra medical and transportation costs when those costs pose a significant burden on that person's ability to lead a, roughly and unambiguously approximated, normal life. Where basic needs are unaffected, for example where the extra costs do not pose a significant burden, compensation would not be a priority. Likewise, the provision of appealing clothes and musical instruments would not be necessary unless there was a case where their provision was deemed vital to the living of a satisfactory life. Yet the provision of more education for those who learn more slowly might well be necessary, assuming that such provision was required to bring people to a basic level. This is due to the fact that a basic level of education is deemed, with good reason, to be conditional for leading a minimally satisfactory life.

So, when Pogge asks 'why even out some natural inequalities but not others?',[20] we can answer, 'because of the impact and ramifications of some natural inequalities, but not others, with respect to people's abilities to lead satisfactory lives'. This entails that we be able to demarcate between basic needs and more superficial, indulgent or less vital wants. It also entails that we be able to determine a level of income above which demand for provision might be said to be audacious. Although these are complex issues, they are resolvable. Moreover, it is uncontroversial to assert that the sorts of claims being discussed here, for example that ramps should be provided for those who rely on wheels to get around, are legitimate compelling claims.

Taking account of natural primary goods more fully when assessing the justice of distributions need not be problematic, then, as Pogge suggests. Consequently, we can reassert that Rawls' semiconsequentialism is unacceptable, given that it fails to take account of contingencies that have a profound impact on people's abilities to take advantage of their social primary goods.

Furthermore, if taking account of natural contingencies is problematic, then taking account of social contingencies would also be likely to be problematic. That is to say, we could rephrase Pogge's question to read 'why even out some social inequalities but not others?' For example, when discussing fair equality of opportunity, Rawls states that 'Chances to acquire cultural knowledge and skills should not depend upon one's class position, and so the school system, whether public or private, should be designed to even out class barriers.'[21] In the style of Pogge, we might ask here just what Rawls' statement requires. Might it require that I be given elocution lessons so that I can speak as if I were from Cheltenham Ladies College, that I be given golf tuition or that I be assigned a daddy who is friends with the director of the London Philharmonic? It is hard to see how such demands could be legitimately ruled out unless an appeal is made to some notion of basic needs. Rawls' difference principle does not come to our assistance, since the principle of fair equality of opportunity is lexically prior to it. Pogge's strategy is indeed to 'narrow the definition of educational opportunities so as to exclude many expensive but not so central items'.[22] That which should then be provided under the principle of fair equality of opportunity is what Pogge calls a minimally adequate education. Two important points present themselves here. The first is that definitions *can* be narrowed. Secondly, if some social inequalities but not others should be evened out because of their impact on 'central' needs, surely some natural inequalities should be evened out too. To compensate for some inequalities but not others when their impacts are similarly severe seems both arbitrary and inconsistent.

There are related difficulties here. The distinction between social and natural contingencies is problematic, as is the task of discerning the relations between them. In addition, there is difficulty defining just what constitutes an advantage as opposed to a disadvantage. For example, some might argue that to speak as if from Cheltenham Ladies College or to be well tutored in golf would be disadvantageous: one could be taken to have a different personality to that which one had, consequently find one's career prospects limited and waste enormous amounts of time in a sand pit (if the tuition didn't pay off). Although (as I will argue later with regard to natural capacities; see Chapter 8, pp. 87–96) there *just do* seem to be things that are advantageous and disadvantageous, the example shows in some cases that it can be difficult to say just what amounts to an advantage as opposed to a disadvantage.

The natural/social distinction is also very difficult to draw. One can question both what is natural with regard to a particular advantage or disadvantage[23] and whether the correspondence between a natural advantage or disadvantage and a social advantage or disadvantage is either direct or inevitable. This became apparent earlier, both in the discussion of blame with regard to relative deprivation and in the discussion of the social aspect of much disability. Assuming there are such things as natural advantages and disadvantages, the relation between them and social advantages and disadvantages can be questioned. Pogge observes that Rawls explains socioeconomic inequalities by reference to two factors, the natural distribution of talents and the prevailing institutional scheme.[24] He argues, however, that this is too simple.

> There is a third factor, namely, how valuable the various natural talents are considered to be in the relevant social system. To some extent this third factor will itself be determined by the prevailing institutional scheme. To some extent it will also be due to exogenous determinants, such as the system's natural environment, culture, and level of development. In any case, this third factor ensures that even so-called *natural* contingencies (the distribution of valuable talents) will have a considerable social component.[25]

..t greater length later (see Chapter 8, pp. 87–96), we should
.. ̇e of the questionable and alterable nature of the relations
..ural and social dis/advantages. Given, then, that it is very diffi-
..aw a clear distinction between natural and social contingencies,
..rgues that it is 'doubtful that a conception of justice can plausibly
..... as much weight on the distinction between natural and social contingencies as Rawls does'.[26] And one advantage of including natural primary goods when thinking about who are the worst off in society is that
these problems are, to a certain extent, circumnavigated. That is to say, it
would be ever so much more important to be extremely precise about distinguishing between natural and social contingencies if we wanted to rule
out one, but not the other, when considering the justice of different distributive schemes.

## Rawls and the worth of liberty distinction

Hitherto, it has been shown that, if we were concerned with the position of
the worst off in society, we would not simply choose a distribution of social
primary goods without taking account of the impact that natural disadvantage might have upon what we could make of such goods. Rawls'
conception of justice can therefore be said to be incomplete in so far as it
fails to sufficiently take account of contingencies that have a profound
impact on people's abilities to lead satisfactory lives. Moreover, with regard
to the principle of fair equality of opportunity, it was shown that it was
inconsistent to compensate for some (social) inequalities but not others
(natural inequalities), when their effects with respect to central needs were
similarly severe. This brings us to our main concern: it is unclear as to why
natural and indeed social inequalities that have severe ramifications with
respect to people's abilities to lead satisfactory lives should not be the concern of Rawls' first principle of justice. We might justly ask, then, whether
liberty can remain unaffected by such inequalities.

As noted earlier, Rawls asserts that 'the fundamental liberties are always
equal'. However, we can question whether that is indeed the case. Returning
to my proposed jump, somersault and painless landing from a second floor
balcony, there are a number of variables that we can introduce. Let us
assume that there is no law against making such a jump. Let us also assume
that I do not own a property with a second floor balcony. I must thereby
pay a levy to a capitalist friend of mine so as to gain access to her balcony.
Assuming that I can pay the levy, whether I can perform my jump, somersault and painless landing will very much depend upon my ability as an
acrobat. If I cannot afford to pay the levy, I will be unable to perform my
jump whether or not I can perform it painlessly. Now in what sense can I be
said to be free to perform my jump, somersault and painless landing if a) I
am physically unable to do it even though I can afford it, b) I am physically
able to do it but cannot afford it, or c) I am physically unable to do it and

cannot afford it? Moreover, in what sense can my liberty be said to be equal to that of a rich acrobat?

Although the liberty at stake here could hardly be said to be funda-mental, the example illustrates the kinds of constraints faced by those on the least-receiving end of natural and social inequalities. We might thereby argue, for example, that if those with special needs can do less with their wealth because of the cost of their needs, then to say that their liberty remains unaffected is insensitive. However, as Scanlon points out, these kinds of constraints on people's abilities to take advantage of their rights do not count as inequalities in liberty for Rawls.[27] Rawls states that

> The inability to take advantage of one's rights and opportunities as a result of poverty and ignorance, and a lack of means generally, is sometimes counted among the constraints definitive of liberty. I shall not, however, say this, but rather I shall think of these things as affect-ing the worth of liberty[28]

So, I may lack the physical and/or fiscal means to perform my somersault without inducing serious injury upon landing, but I am indeed free to complete the jump without pain. It is just that that freedom means very little to me. Here then, meaningless or worthless freedoms are freedoms all the same and, while this enables Rawls to maintain that we can all be said to be free, it is far from obvious as to why we should accept such a mini-malistic conception of human freedom. If we should reject such a concep-tion, then we should likewise reject the idea that we can all be said to be free, let alone equally so.

Rawls' idea is that his first principle of justice guarantees equal liberty for all and his second principle maximises the worth of liberty to the least advantaged.

> Freedom as equal liberty is the same for all; the question of compen-sating for a less than equal liberty does not arise. But the worth of lib-erty is not the same for everyone. Some have greater authority and wealth, and therefore greater means to achieve their aims. The lesser worth of liberty is, however, compensated for, since the capacity of the less fortunate members of society to achieve their aims would be even less were they not to accept the existing inequalities whenever the dif-ference principle is satisfied ... Taking the two principles together, the basic structure is to be arranged to maximize the worth to the least advantaged of the complete scheme of equal liberty shared by all.[29]

This passage does not seem to mention the influence of natural con-tingencies, such as physical ability, on freedom, although one would think that they would be considered as partly comprising the possession or 'lack of means generally'. This is hardly surprising given that, as we have seen,

Rawls excludes natural contingencies when considering who are the worst off in society. The passage does, however, deny that wealth directly affects freedom (and we have seen the influence that natural contingencies can have on what we can do with our wealth). Wealth, then, is only said to affect the worth of freedom – not freedom itself.

Pogge construes Rawls' conception of the worth of freedom as a function of three components:

> the public recognition of certain basic freedoms ... their protection ... and the means at one's disposal ... Let us say that the first component determines (formal) legal freedom; that the first two components together determine effective legal freedom (Rawls: freedom); and that all three components together determine worth of freedom or ... worth-while freedom.[30]

He argues that, while the third component is dealt with by the second principle of justice, the first principle governs both of the other components, 'reflecting the realization that basic rights and liberties protect our freedom only insofar as they are themselves well-protected, that is, upheld and enforced'.[31]

Asserting that Rawls' lexically prior first principle is attempting to guarantee effective legal freedom means that we are granted more than paper freedoms under that principle. An example of a paper freedom would be where I have the right to do $x$ and you sit on me, thereby stopping me from doing $x$. My right to do $x$ is not effective in this case, even though on paper that right is guaranteed. The significance of Rawls' first principle guaranteeing effective legal freedom is that you will be prevented from sitting on me; my right to do $x$ will be protected. However, excluding the third component (the means at one's disposal) from the first principle of justice entails that, while effective legal freedom amounts to more than paper freedom in one sense, it amounts to no more than paper freedom in another. That is to say, if I have the right to do $x$ but I cannot afford to do $x$, my right to do $x$ is still legally effective even though I cannot do $x$. So, Rawls' first principle ensures that you cannot hold me back but it allows that my situation can hold me back. A potential consequence of this is that, as Pogge aptly notes, the integrity of our person is protected against violence while it collapses through deprivation of food and shelter.[32] We must thereby ask whether Rawls is right to attach so much more importance to effective legal freedom than he does to worthwhile freedom.

Pogge argues that the rationale behind attaching overriding importance to effective legal freedom is that, even though it is the case that the extent to which one is in a position to enjoy one's freedoms is a function of one's wealth and income, without publicly recognised and effectively enforced basic rights, the enjoyment of the correlative freedoms is altogether out of the question.[33] It is questionable, however, whether those in the worst off position in society would always want an extension of their effective legal freedoms instead of some increase in their means for enjoying such liberties. As Pogge notes, Rawls needs to show that for each basic liberty, L, having L is lexically more important than having the means for enjoyment of the freedom L protects, and that having L is lexically more important than the means for the enjoyment of any first principle freedom.[34] This entails that he would have to deny the following possibility:

> that a greater gain in the worthwhile freedom of the poor would result from an improvement in their income and education (enabling them better to take advantage of their existing basic rights and liberties) than from additional legal rights (whose effect on their worthwhile freedom may be rather slight so long as they remain poor and uneducated).[35]

Yet Rawls' formulation seems to constitute just such a denial when he states that 'a departure from the institutions of equal liberty required by the first principle cannot be justified by, or compensated for, by greater social and economic advantages'.[36] Rawls takes the basic liberties of citizens to be, 'roughly speaking':

> political liberty (the right to vote and to be eligible for public office) together with freedom of speech and assembly; liberty of conscience and freedom of thought; freedom of the person along with the right to hold (personal) property; and freedom from arbitrary arrest and seizure as defined by the concept of the rule of law.[37]

Contra Rawls, it is at the very least insensitive to suggest that those leading relatively impoverished lives would or should prefer, say, an extension of their rights of assembly to the provision of some blankets for the winter months. As Pogge argues, Rawls' insistence on the pre-eminence of the basic civil and political rights and liberties constitutes a denial of the fundamental role that basic social and economic needs actually play in a human life.[38] We need not accept such a denial.

Rawls could be said to take a wrong turn, then, when he assigns lexical priority to a principle that guarantees more than paper rights in one sense (effective legal freedom) but guarantees no more than paper rights in another (no minimum worth of liberty). Such a principle fails to be sensitive to the profundity of the influence of social (and natural) contingencies on freedom. If jumping from a second floor balcony suddenly became a fundamental liberty deemed to have a crucial role in self-development, for example, it is unlikely that anyone would choose to be assigned an abstract right to jump from a third floor balcony in preference to being given the money to gain access to the second floor balcony and to undergo the training, if required, to *actually make* such a jump. However, Rawls asserts that the idea of incorporating a guaranteed minimum of means at one's disposal into the first principle of justice is superfluous. 'Whatever the merits of this suggestion, it is superfluous in view of the difference principle. For any fraction of the index of primary goods enjoyed by the least advantaged can already be regarded in this manner.'[39] While this is clearly true in an ideal situation, where the difference principle is satisfied, it is not true in a non-ideal situation,[40] for example, where the first principle of justice is yet to be satisfied. Thus, as Pogge points out, a possible strategy for Rawls is to emphasise the design priority (in ideal situations) of the first principle of justice while denying the implementation priority of it (in non-ideal situations).[41]

Although it is a possible strategy for Rawls to restrict the lexical priority of his principles of justice to ideal theory, it is not a strategy that he seems to adopt.

> Viewing the theory of justice as a whole, the ideal part presents a conception of a just society that we are to achieve if we can. Existing institutions are to be judged in the light of this conception … The lexical ranking of the principles specifies which elements of the ideal are relatively more urgent, and the priority rules this ordering suggests are to be applied to nonideal cases as well … Thus while the principles of justice belong to the theory of an ideal state of affairs, they are generally relevant.[42]

We are still left, then, with the unacceptable possibility that 'meeting basic social and economic needs will in nonideal contexts take second place to the establishment of basic liberties (which could hardly be enjoyed by those whose basic needs remain unmet)'.[43] Other strategies open to Rawls so as to avoid this unacceptable possibility are discussed in depth by Pogge. Two of them are summarised here.

One such strategy is for Rawls to incorporate a limitation on economic inequalities into his first principle of justice. This idea, as Pogge notes, draws upon the requirement that is already part of the first principle, that the fair value of the basic political liberties be protected.[44] So, where Rawls writes that 'those similarly endowed and motivated should have roughly the same chance of attaining positions of political authority irrespective of their economic and social class',[45] we might infer a proviso ruling out radical economic inequalities so that those similarly endowed do have roughly the same chance. However, to rule out radical inequality would be to rule in a guaranteed minimum, something that we have seen Rawls reject as superfluous. Moreover, as Pogge argues, Rawls assumes that the fair value of the basic political liberties will be protected through the 'public financing of political campaigns and election expenditures, various limits on contributions and other regulations'.[46] Such a narrow interpretation of his first principle does not provide Rawls with a way of avoiding the unacceptable possibility detailed above.

Another problem-avoiding strategy is for Rawls both to assert that his serial ordering only applies in reasonably favourable conditions[47] and to deny that the aforementioned unacceptable possibility is a possibility in such conditions. He states, for example, that

> in adopting a serial order we are in effect making a special assumption in the original position, namely, that the parties know that the conditions of their society, whatever they are, admit the effective realization of the equal liberties.[48]

A consequence of this however would be that, given that basic social and economic needs have been shown to be unmet, reasonably favourable conditions do not obtain in our society. Pogge argues that this would 'frustrate Rawls' hope that his theory can provide definite political guidance for institutional reform under existing conditions'.[49] Moreover, according to Pogge, the 'unacceptable possibility' *is* a possibility in reasonably favourable conditions, even truly favourable conditions:

> A social system under truly favourable conditions is presumably advanced enough economically to *render feasible* economic institutions under which the most urgent needs are met, but the feasibility of such institutions hardly entails their existence. Those in the worst socioeconomic position may *in fact* be malnourished, illiterate and destitute ... The hypothesis that *if* the United States had a just economy then all could fully exercise their basic liberties suffices to trigger the serial ordering, regardless of the extent to which the real existing poor can in fact take advantage of their basic liberties. [50]

It is hard to see, then, how Rawls can theoretically avoid the possibility, which we need not accept, 'of an underclass of destitute persons living in a society that is economically advanced enough to bring into play the serial ordering of the two principles'[51] whereupon the basic social and economic needs of some would (in non-ideal situations) take second place to the fulfilment of the first principle of justice. We can thereby assert that Rawls is wrong to attach so much more importance to effective legal freedom than he does to worthwhile freedom. Indeed, we might argue that Rawls is wrong to state that the fundamental liberties are always equal.

We need not accept such a limited conception of human freedom as that articulated by Rawls in his first principle of justice. It is the claim that a worthless freedom is a freedom nonetheless that lands Rawls with the difficulties outlined above. Such a claim fails to sufficiently recognise the importance of social and natural contingencies. It could be said to amount to a rather irreverent use of the term 'freedom', for it allows one to hold that everyone in society is equally free while some may not be in a position to meet their basic social and economic needs, a fundamental prerequisite for a minimally worthwhile human life.[52] Using the term in this way does not seem to match the moral gravity that is usually attached to it. Yet this is, in effect, what Rawls does. Due to the fact that worthlessness is not ruled out, effective legal freedom is a very minimal and sometimes quite meaningless concept of freedom, which in turn renders specious the claim that we should have a right to the most extensive total system of equal basic liberties. Rawls' first principle, then, is rather an empty gesture.[53]

The arguments so far suggest instead that the worth of liberty distinction, as Rawls draws it, is mistaken. Rather, it should be acknowledged that, in order to meaningfully describe something as a freedom, some degree of worth must be present. That is to say, social and natural contingencies should be seen as among the constraints *definitive* of liberty.[54] If that were the case, a freedom would have to be to some extent worthwhile or realisable so as to be rightly articulated as such. And, given that at least *some* degree of worth would thereby be stipulated, the worth of liberty distinction would then become operative so as to determine the *degree* of worth of a given freedom. If this were to be acknowledged, then it would follow that those whose basic social and economic needs remain unmet cannot be said to be free. It would follow in turn that the claim that the fundamental liberties are always equal is false.

It has been contended throughout this section that a concept of liberty would do well to be sensitive to the influence of both natural and social contingencies on freedom. This is best done, as I suggest below, by abandoning the blanket assumption of negative liberty coupled with the worth of liberty clause as Rawls articulates it. In so far as Rawls' conception of liberty ignores natural inequalities and admits of worthless freedoms, we were right to be uncomfortable with it.

## Realisable freedom

It has been shown that natural primary goods should be included in the equation determining who are the worst off in society and that a conception of justice should be sensitive to the influence of natural and social contingencies on freedom. Given this, it is more fitting to make a distinction between legal freedom and a more inclusive or realisable freedom and to acknowledge that realisable freedom is conditional upon ability, whether physical, fiscal or both.[55] This ensures that worthless freedoms in the Rawlsian sense are clearly demarcated from realisable freedom and lends support to the intuitively appealing idea that one cannot be said in any meaningful sense to be free to do that which one is unable to do.

The example of the person in a wheelchair at the bottom of a flight of stairs will illustrate how freedom is inextricably linked with ability if the concept is to have any meaning to the agent to whom it is meant to apply.

Let us assume that the person in a wheelchair is unable to climb stairs. Yet, on the negative conception, she is free to do so. Freedom here means nothing to the agent due to their inability to realise it. Contrast this with a person in a wheelchair at the bottom of a ramp. They are, on the negative conception, free to move up the ramp and this freedom is realisable in so far as they *can* move up the ramp. The difference between the two freedoms in this case is immense and remains unaccounted for by the negative model. The former freedom is not only worthless; it is not a freedom in anything like the same sense as the latter. It seems to make much more sense, then, to demarcate between legal or hypothetical freedom and realisable freedom. If one is legally free to do *x* but unable to do *x*, one is only legally free. If one is legally free to do *x* and able to do *x*, freedom is realisable. Likewise, if one is effectively prohibited from doing *x* but able to do *x*, one has no freedom and only hypothetical ability; and if one is effectively prohibited from doing *x* and unable to do *x*, one has neither freedom nor ability. Thus, a legal or hypothetical freedom cannot be realised without ability and ability cannot be realised without freedom.

Now while the importance of legal or hypothetical freedom should be acknowledged given that it is a condition of freedom's realisation, it is realisable freedom that is the stuff of value. Worthless freedom is rarely subject to demand. Rather, it is the idea that freedom has practical manifestation which explains why it means such a lot to us – why it is cherished, fought for and taken away as a punishment. So, in the interests of our concept of freedom matching up with the value we attach to freedom, it should be recognised as being conditional on ability.[56] To claim that *x* is free to do *y* when *y* is unable to do *y* renders freedom relatively meaningless in a lot of contexts and to a lot of people. Equating freedom with ability on the other hand is more sympathetic to our intuitions about the value of liberty and ensures that the term cannot be used as a potentially rather insensitive conceptual veneer.

The idea that freedom cannot be realised without ability has further ramifications in that it admits that there can be many more constraints on an agent's freedom than simply 'external impediments of motion'. Whatever hinders our ability by implication hinders our freedom. Excluding lots of things as counting as limitations, by definition, is no longer justifiable.[57] And Feinberg argues that, once we realise that constraints to freedom can be internal (for example, compulsive desires or ignorance) and also negative (such as poverty or a lack of strength), we can dispense with the positive–negative liberty distinction.

> A constraint is something – anything – that prevents one from doing something. Therefore, if nothing prevents me from doing x, I am free to do x; conversely, if I am free to do x, then nothing prevents me from doing x. 'Freedom to' and 'freedom from' are in this way logically linked, and there can be no special 'positive freedom' to, which is not also a 'freedom from'.[58]

Thus, negative liberty theory only articulates part of what it means to be free. A more comprehensive definition of freedom is provided by Gerald MacCallum, who argues that underlying both positive and negative conceptions of freedom is the same concept of liberty. He expresses this in the triadic formula; '$x$ is (is not) free from $y$ to do (not do, become, not become) $z$'.[59] Such a formula attempts to elicit as simply as possible what freedom is without prior judgement as to what freedoms are important or what counts as unfreedom. It follows from this that 'differences of opinion over liberty, turn on different interpretations of what (for the purposes of freedom), counts as an agent, a constraint or an objective'.[60] And the arguments so far suggest that inability should count as a constraint upon freedom. When we are free in the meaningful sense of the word, we are necessarily free to do something whether we do it or not. To do something requires that we are able to do it. Therefore, inability is a source of unfreedom.

Given that inability is a source of unfreedom, deprivation can be seen to be a source of unfreedom too. Impairment-induced disability can be seen as a restriction of ability and thus freedom, due to functional limitation. Likewise, the social aspect of disability and relative social deprivation can be seen as restrictions upon freedom. Applying MacCallum's formula, it seems fairly uncontroversial that a relatively deprived person or a person with an impairment should count as an agent, that economic, political, social, legal, environmental and interpersonal obstacles (or failures) should count as constraints and that living a life that is to some definable extent worthwhile and comfortable should count as an objective. It is these latter restrictions of freedom that are especially important to political theory due to the fact that they are socially determined. The situation is alterable, if not eradicable. By implication, then, our theoretical position should account for the fact that people who are relatively deprived and people with impairments have their freedom limited in many ways and that this unfreedom is, to a significant extent, socially determined. Moreover, it should provide a justification as to why the situation is not altered so as to increase the freedom of those people.

Before asking why it is that we do not bother to alter a socially determined situation of unfreedom, that the corresponding freedoms are worth bothering about has to be established. One of the consequences of recognising the dependency of being free to do something on the ability to do it is that the sphere of unfreedom is broadened. Although it can now be asserted, for example, that a person in a wheelchair at the bottom of a flight of stairs is not free to climb them, it can also be said that neither am I free to eat my computer, jump half a mile into the air or drink fine wine on Jupiter tonight. As a result, the argument might run, the idea of unfreedom is cheapened: it no longer counts for the same as it did under the negative Rawlsian conception. Negative liberty theory rules out superficial claims to unfreedom at the point of definition. I am not unfree to jump half a mile into the air because nobody is stopping me. However, as we have seen, it also rules out many serious incapacities as being concerns of human freedom. In the interests of not doing this, the sphere of unfreedom has been broadened. Yet this need not entail that all unfreedoms are as serious as each other and, by implication, that all objectives are of equal value. Rather, it is a question of deciding which freedoms we should be able to enjoy and which abilities we should be free to exercise.[61]

Certain activities are valued over others and the freedoms facilitating their exercise are of corresponding importance. For example, work, travel, social interaction, education, sport and shopping seem to be valued over and above eating computers, jumping half a mile into the air and drinking fine wine on Jupiter. This goes some way to explain why offices, roads, bars, schools, football stadiums and shopping centres are in greater evidence than edible computers, jet-propelled boots or flights to Jupiter. We have deemed such activities, rightly or wrongly, to be of value and the corresponding freedoms to be worth facilitating and protecting. To be unfree to do these things is therefore more serious than to be unfree to do other more superficial (or ridiculous) things. Moreover, it is clear that the kinds of freedoms denied to people who find themselves socially deprived in one way or another are indeed those that are generally deemed by society to be worth granting and protecting. Given this, to argue that people who find themselves without a home should have limited freedom with regard to health, access to services, employment and participation in the community would be either hypocritical or wildly discriminatory. So would it be to argue that people with impairments should have limited freedom with regard to education, employment, travel, leisure and social interaction. Furthermore, the kinds of freedoms denied to people who are socially deprived are important basic freedoms upon which the enjoyment of other valuable or more superficial freedoms is conditional. Freedoms with regard to housing, education, health, employment and travel, for example, are foundational to the experience of other freedoms as well as being highly valued in themselves. Without them, we could not even entertain thoughts of jet-propelled boots or flights to Jupiter. Nor would there be much left of social and professional life as we presently recognise and enjoy it. So, the fact that such freedoms are freedoms upon which so many other pursuits depend entails that to be denied them constitutes a profound impediment.

Given that the kinds of objectives that people who suffer social deprivations are unfree to pursue are the kinds of objectives that society considers to be worthwhile to be free to pursue, we may justly ask why such freedoms are not facilitated or protected in these cases. That such freedoms are conditional to the enjoyment of many other freedoms makes the question all the more important. One possible answer would be to cite the inconsistency of government. Adversarial, ad hoc and incremental policy with little underpinning philosophy goes some way in explaining the continuation of the social aspect of disability and relative social deprivation. In no way, however, does it provide a justification of the resulting inequality of human freedom. Similarly, and specifically with regard to disability, our impoverished understanding can explain, but in no way justify, social disadvantage and unfreedom. Misrepresentations of people with impairments as deviant, morally unequal, 'invalid' charity cases, to say the least, detract from initiatives in support of the provision of basic freedoms.[62] And it is interesting to note the relationship here between legislation and social understanding in so far as progress in social understanding could be catalytic to legislative change and vice versa.

Another explanation could be that, in practice, the government has greater financial priorities than tackling social deprivation. Projects deemed to be of more importance and other political commitments, when coupled with finite resources, often go some way to explain continuing social inadequacies. Once again, however, that money is not spent on redressing social injustice does not justify that it not be spent. What is interesting about this possible explanation is that it brings to our attention the fact that money would have to be spent in order to eradicate both relative social deprivation and socially induced disability. It is from this requirement that subtleties concerning responsibility for unfreedom evolve.

Many paradigm cases of unfreedom simply entail the removal of an obstacle for their resolution. In addition, somebody is usually held responsible for removing the said obstacle due to the fact that they imposed it. For example, if $a$ drives his car into my path, then I ($x$) am not free from this automotive constraint ($y$) to reach my destination ($z$). If $a$ removes his car ($y$), then my freedom is restored and, since it was he who put it there, he can be held responsible for removing it. This is a simple case where an obstacle is imposed upon a prior state of freedom and responsibility for its removal can be easily identified. Unfortunately, cases of unfreedom are not always this simple.

If $a$ parked his car in what was to be my path an hour before I showed up, I am still prevented from reaching my destination but the situation is not the same. I might not know that it is $a$'s car, but assuming I do, I might justifiably ask him to remove it. If he fails to remove this obstacle, I might feel unjustly treated, especially if he put it there with the intention of constraining my freedom. Here, then, failure to remove an obstacle ($y$) is the problem, the seriousness of which depends upon whether it was intentionally placed there.

Now let us suppose that I have not taken this path to my destination ($z$) for some time or always thought it out of bounds. I am told that my intentions will be thwarted since there is a car ($y$) across the path. It has been there for a long time, has rusted and become immovable; it even looks like part of the landscape these days. After further investigation, I find out that it could have been $a$'s car although nobody is sure. Even if it were $a$'s car, he moved to Jupiter some years ago. The local authority inform me that they could remove the car ($y$) but it would have little priority due to the cost of the project coupled with the fact that they did not put the car there and so it is not really their responsibility. Moreover, even if they took the car away, the path would have to be reconstructed so as to right the damage and meet new specifications, something that is beyond their call of duty. Here, then, $y$ becomes the non-negotiable path and there would seem to be nobody that I can hold responsible for providing me with a route to my destination ($z$).

All of these examples are cases of unfreedom, the moral severities of which are held to descend in importance. That some of the unfreedoms endured by socially disabled people fall into the category deemed to be of least importance would go some way to explain why such unfreedoms continue to be endured. That much social 'reconstruction' would be required in the case of relative social deprivation, so as to make paths that many of us take for granted negotiable to others, is similarly obvious. There is little declared intention with regard to the generation of relative deprivation and, correspondingly, little assumption of responsibility for its alleviation. So, we need to look at what is required both to liberate people from relative social deprivation and to liberate people from the social aspect of disability.

Taking the social aspect of disability first, in some cases all that is required is the removal of obstacles that constrain people's freedom, whether put there intentionally or misguidedly. Desegregation of schools and elimination of discrimination in the workplace, for example, would extend the freedom of people with impairments with regard to education and employment. Here, then, removal of obstacles (segregation and discrimination) is enough to secure freedom. Likewise, we could argue that, given awareness of the requirements of people who rely on wheels to negotiate their environment, to erect a new building without ramps would be to impose an obstacle upon the freedom of those people. However, the difference in this case (assuming that stairs would be the obstacle to entry) is that to remove the obstacle (stairs) would not secure freedom. Here, then, $x$ would not be free if $y$ were removed: the obstacle is only part of the problem.

With regard to people who are relatively deprived, the obstacles to their freedom are in the main negative. That is to say, they are a lack of things like shelter, adequate housing, jobs and respectable welfare. We might argue that to eliminate stigmatisation would encourage more respect and more self-respect but, as in the case of socially induced disability, obstacles are generally only part of the problem. Unsurprisingly, to remove what shelter there is, knock down egregious housing estates and eradicate welfare would not secure freedom.

When the removal of $y$ is enough to secure freedom in a given case, the conditions other than $y$ must be, by implication, conditions of freedom. When removal of $y$ does not secure freedom, a state of unfreedom prior to (or without) the imposition of $y$ is implied. The latter situation is evident in many cases where relatively deprived people and people with impairments find their freedom curtailed. For example, inadequate housing and inadequate welfare provision can both be seen to constrain the freedom of people who are relatively socially deprived. Likewise, inaccessible public transport, inadequate care provision and the prevalence of stairs can all be seen to constrain the freedom of people with impairments. So, buses, shelters, welfare measures and stairs, as they are, constrain the freedom of some people. Yet to take them away would not leave anybody with more freedom (except perhaps the taxpayer). The offending constraints either have to be replaced or improved, or their removal must be complemented with some sort of provision.

The vital requirement, then, to remedy limitations of freedom with regard to many instances of social deprivation is not just that obstacles are removed but that something is provided. Indeed, obstacles might cease to be obstacles in some cases, once augmented by some kind of provision. The level of such provision, so as to secure conditional basic liberties, is open to question. That is to say, we need to attain a sensible conception of what constitutes an acceptable degree of worth that in turn denotes that a freedom is indeed realisable.[63] However, the fact that *some* provision is required supplies more ammunition to those wishing to dodge responsibility. They need no longer rest their case with the argument that obstacles to the freedom of people who are socially deprived have never been intentionally imposed by society (we weren't aware, for example, that disability had such a strong social component) and that, as a result, failure to remove them does not entail moral condemnation. It could further be argued that, even if obstacles to freedom were removed, society would have to make all sorts of provisions to secure freedom for those who find themselves deprived and that the failure to provide for freedom is in no way the same as taking it away. This position could be held to provide a justification as to why society does not feel obligated either to provide for freedom in the general case of relative social deprivation or to provide for freedom in the more specific case of disability. To discover whether it is indeed such a justification requires an investigation into the nature and moral relevance of the distinction between imposing obstacles to freedom and failing to provide for it. Part Two of the book couches this investigation in terms of the question of the difference between harming and failing to help.

# Part Two

# Methods of evasion

## Introduction

Given that some sort of provision would be required to secure freedom for people who are socially deprived, this section will look at just how serious it is to fail to provide.

The term 'social exclusion', while fashionable, tends to imply that society is deliberately setting out to exclude people, which is an unfair assumption with which to proceed. It might be permissible to say that social practices are *exclusionary*, in that they have the effect of excluding, but to assert that the effect of excluding is the deliberate result of human action could be said to be philosophically evasive. At the very least, the term 'exclusion' is quite easily mixed up with the idea that we are *doing* something bad. And while it seems coherent to say that we can exclude unintentionally, the idea that we are not doing much at all, that we are failing to include, reflects more clearly the lack of agency involved in the issues we are dealing with (whether or not the effect is best described as exclusionary or non-inclusive). Indeed, it is pertinent to the issue of social deprivation that we acknowledge that we are doing nothing or, at least, very little. Hence, the approach taken here is to investigate the moral seriousness of the somewhat weaker and arguably more accurate claim that society is merely failing to include. To show that 'mere failure', or non-inclusion, is morally reprehensible is a far more challenging line of inquiry and, if successful, provides a more precise and robust critique of current social practices.

The idea, then, that the failure to provide is less morally serious than actively harming, that we are merely failing to include as opposed to setting out to socially exclude, is a potential justification for the continued failure to provide. That idea will be scrutinised in the following chapter and it will be shown to have significant shortcomings. Another method of evasion with respect to cases of social deprivation is to argue that the unfreedoms endured are in no way intended, if indeed they are foreseen. Such an argument generally appeals to the doctrine or principle of double effect. The doctrine of double effect will thereby be investigated so as to discern what we can legitimately be said to intend and how the notion of intention upsets the distinction between harming and failing to help. Other considerations that affect the justifiability of a given situation of harm will then be discussed. How they, along with consideration of intention, specifically apply with regard to the failure to provide in the cases of relative social deprivation and socially induced disability will be described. A libertarian method of evasion will then be discussed and it will be shown to have serious weaknesses. It will be concluded both that the failure to provide in cases of social deprivation is morally serious and that the methods of evading responsibility discussed do not justify the continuation of that failure. It will also be shown how the arguments appealed to throughout this section cohere with the justification of the commonly accepted ideal of democracy.

# 4 The doing/allowing distinction

The distinction between imposing obstacles to freedom and failing to provide for it correlates with the distinction between harming and failing to help. In this chapter we will see that the conceptual distinction between harming and failing to help can be drawn. It is usually drawn with a view to making the further moral claim that harming is worse than failing to help. However, some cases of failing to help suggest otherwise. One strategy is to bracket those cases in with cases of harming. I will argue that this is mistaken. It will become apparent that there are many more morally relevant factors requiring consideration in cases of harm than simply whether they came about by action or inaction. In what follows, it will be shown that the failure to rectify a situation of harm cannot be excused solely by reference to its not being actively inflicted. Likewise, unfreedom is not always justified by the claim that it has not been imposed.

The imposition of limitations on freedom, assuming that the freedom in question is valued, is an example of the doing of harm. It further implies a prior state of freedom, that there is something to be impeded. (If it does not imply a prior state of freedom, the restriction, to count as a restriction, must be a further restriction to one already encountered.) Failure to remove limitations on freedom, assuming that the freedom in question is valued, is an example of the allowing of harm or the failure to help. It further implies a prior state of unfreedom in that something is required to secure it. Great moral relevance is accorded to the above distinction by some writers. Imposing limits on freedom or doing harm is deemed to be more serious than failing to provide for freedom or allowing harm. And while this seems to suit our intuitions so well in many cases, the emphasis on this distinction does not provide a complete picture. It could be held, for instance, to conflict with the idea that unfreedom or harm is bad whether done or allowed, or the notion that the reasons not to harm provide the very reasons why we should help. We can ask, then, why it is that imposing obstacles or doing harm is held to be worse than failing to remove obstacles or allowing harm.

Let us suppose that there is a limitation $x$ to our freedom which cannot be held to have been imposed at any time or for any reason. Given the importance of the freedom impeded by $x$, it is decided that the limitation should be removed and it is so removed. Having said this, it would only be a case of allowing unfreedom had we failed to remove the constraint. Now let us suppose that after enjoying a period of freedom from $x$ to do $y$, it is decided that $x$ should be replaced and it is so replaced as an obstacle. The restoration of $x$ becomes an imposition of a constraint and, in so far as the curtailment of freedom is seen to be bad, the doing of harm. Given that $x$ has not changed throughout the sequence of events, we must ask what it is about the latter situation of unfreedom that makes it more morally serious than the former. There is no difference between them other than that one is allowed and the other initiated. Moreover, if the unfreedom had simply continued to be allowed, it would still exist but escape moral outcry.

This scenario can be applied to the case of socially induced disability if we consider, for example, $x$ to be a ramp-free environment. (It also applies to the case of relative social deprivation if, for example, we substitute ramps for homes or decent hostels.) Suppose that ramps were built so that wheelchair users could access the built environment and after a year or so were removed. There would rightly be outrage at that removal due to perception of the resulting hardship. Here, illustration of the hardship provides the reason as to why ramps should be built: thought of the harm gives reason to help. Furthermore, the harm is no different from the situation now where ramps are sparse. Why then do we not build them? Adherence to the doing/allowing distinction entails that failing to build ramps is less morally reprehensible than knocking them down. There must therefore be something particularly morally abhorrent about doing harm which increases the harm through virtue of its origin.

A notable exposition of the idea that doing harm is indeed more serious than allowing it is provided by Warren S. Quinn.[1] I take Quinn here as a representative example of those who support this position or something like it. Quinn adopts the idea that action is a matter of the presence of something and inaction a matter of its absence. From this he makes a distinction between 'harmful positive agency' and 'harmful negative agency':

> the distinction between harm occurring because of what the agent does (because of the existence of one of his actions) and harm occurring because of what the agent did not do but might have done (because of the non instantiation of some kind of action that he might have performed).[2]

Having made this distinction, Quinn goes on to refine it so as to deal with difficult cases where inaction has more sinister implications. One such difficult case is his 'Rescue III'.

> We are off by special train to save five who are in imminent danger of death. Every second counts. You have just taken over from the driver, who has left the locomotive to attend to something. Since the train is

on automatic control you need do nothing to keep it going. But you can stop it by putting on the brakes. You suddenly see someone trapped ahead on the track. Unless you act he will be killed. But if you stop, and then free the man, the rescue mission will be aborted. So you let the train continue.[3]

Quinn argues here that we should stop the train simply because we can stop the train from killing the one. If we do not, 'the train kills the man because of your intention that it continue forward'. Here then, the distinction between intentional and foreseen allowing of harm is introduced, to the effect that only foreseen allowing of harm counts as harmful negative agency.

The combination of control and intention in 'Rescue III' makes for a certain kind of complicity. Your choice to let the train go forward is strategic and deliberate. Since you clearly would have it continue for the sake of the five, there is a sense in which, by deliberately not stopping it, you do have it continue. For these reasons your agency counts as positive.[4]

Where inaction is deliberate so as to cause harm, then, Quinn calls it positive agency.

To the idea of positive agency by action, we must therefore add positive agency by this special kind of inaction ... that is, where harm comes from an active object or force, an agent may by inaction contribute the harmful action of the object itself ... Harmful positive agency is that in which an agent's most direct contribution to the harm is an action, whether his own or that of some object.[5]

Quinn seems to think, then, that the doing/allowing distinction has something to offer with the proviso that cases of intentional allowing count as cases of doing. This proviso suits our intuitions about some cases of allowing harm but we must ask whether this is the right way to satisfy our intuitions. That is to say, can negative agency in some circumstances really become positive agency or is this an elaborate terminological manoeuvre with the hope of saving the moral distinction between doing and allowing? Consideration of the 'Trolley Problem' will help us here.

Quinn is anxious to show that the Trolley Problem does not upset his definitions of positive and negative agency. The scene is set with a runaway trolley threatening five people trapped on the track on which it is moving. They will die if the driver does nothing but be saved if the driver switches to a sidetrack on which one person is trapped. There seems ample reason here for the driver to switch tracks yet making the switch would seem to count as the more reprehensible positive agency as opposed to the purportedly less reprehensible alternative of doing nothing. Quinn deals with this seemingly problematic counterexample by asserting that the driver's passive option, letting the train continue on the track, is really a form of positive agency:

> This is because the only possibly acceptable reasons for him not to switch would be to prevent the death of the man on the sidetrack or to keep clean hands. But the clean-hands motive begs the question; it presupposes that the doctrine does not also speak against not switching. So in deciding the status of his possible inaction we must put this motive aside. This leaves the aim of preventing the death of the man on the side-track. But if the driver fails to switch for this reason, it is because he intends that the train continue in a way that will save the man. But then he intends that the train continue forward past the switch, and this leads to the death of the five. So, by my earlier definitions, his choice is really between two different positive options – one passive and one active. And that is why he may pick the alternative that does less harm.[6]

Quinn's solution here is far from convincing. It is hard to see how doing nothing can be called positive agency without redefining doing nothing as doing something. It seems to make much more sense to say that doing nothing in the case of the runaway trolley is indeed negative agency but that there are good reasons in this case to take the positive step of switching tracks. This of course would be to upset the emphasis against doing as opposed to allowing harm, but that is arguably inevitable. For there genuinely to be two positive options, as Quinn asserts, we would have to modify the Trolley Problem. Just suppose, for example, that the driver is on a middle track between the track with the five trapped on it and the track with the one trapped on it. He can switch to either track but, if he continues on the middle track, the trolley will hurtle into a shed full of dynamite and explode, killing everyone. Here the driver really would seem to be presented with two positive options (and a less compelling negative one). To be consistent, Quinn would have to argue that there were three positive options in the amended example, but this goes against our common-sense idea of doing as opposed to not doing. His terminological manoeuvre can thus be said to beg the question itself since it presupposes that positive agency is worse than negative agency and then defines reprehensible negative agency as positive agency so as to prove it.

If Quinn abandoned the rather paradoxical redefinition of intentional negative agency as positive agency, his position would collapse into the more simple and accurate assertion that negative agency is in some cases unjustifiable (as in the case of the runaway trolley) and in some cases there may be good reason and justification for positive agency (as in the case of the runaway trolley). That seems a lot more straightforward – and avoids potentially endless redefinitions of what it is to do and allow so as to cope with troublesome counter examples as they crop up or are created.

Furthermore, such an approach copes better with historical relativity as to what constitutes harm or, more commonly, justified harm. In theory, to retain such a strong emphasis against doing as opposed to allowing harm, we would have to redescribe activities to conform to shifts in their acceptability if we wanted to acquit ourselves of any wrongdoing. That is, if this is really the way we should discern the morality of events, then, given that what we think is morally acceptable has changed and does change, we would have to get up to all sorts of creative accounting to stay faithful to the acts/omissions distinction over time. For example, dressing up rather nicely and chasing a fox on horseback around the English countryside, armed with a bugle and a pack of dogs, has recently been banned by the British government. It would seem hard to contend that the activity was not harmful up to the time of legislation and now it is. Any fox would dispute that. And it would seem equally hard to contend that fox hunting up to the time of legislation was harmful negative agency and so permitted, but now it is harmful positive agency and so ruled out. Rather, it is much more simple to say that it has always been harmful positive agency but that we can no longer find a sustainable justification for it. The point is that it is more accurate and less problematic to contend that what counts as harm or acceptable harm and, as a result, what actions and inactions are justified, may have changed over the course of history than it is to contend that what counts as action and inaction or doing and allowing has so changed. Knowledge that some disability is socially induced, for example, may very well draw to our attention the remediable nature of the unfreedom endured. It may even make allowing such unfreedom to continue unjustifiable. It would be inaccurate, however, to redefine our negative agency with regard to the continuation of events as positive agency. We are still doing nothing.

All of these arguments suggest that the moral appraisal of a given outcome does not rest solely on whether it came about through action or inaction, that becoming creative about how we categorise acts and omissions is a dubious way of trying to save the distinction and that, instead, our focus should be more towards the outcome itself rather than how it came about. Indeed, as a further illustration, at the time of writing there is growing concern about an impending humanitarian disaster in Niger, which governments in a position to help are doing little if anything about. The distinction between acts and omissions seems almost completely insignificant in such a context. Moreover, it seems as misguided to suggest that we are *doing* something terrible as it is to suggest that our failure to do anything is morally acceptable. And with this situation in mind, it is easy to share Jonathan Glover's concern that 'it may well be because of tacit acceptance of the acts and omissions doctrine that we acquiesce in the worst evils in the world'.[7]

The approach developed here suggests that we should not retain such a strong moral emphasis on the distinction between positive and negative agency. Doing harm can be justified and allowing harm unjustified in certain circumstances. Given, then, that the moral evaluation of a given situation of harm is not solely determined by whether it came about through action or inaction, sole appeal to the distinction between doing and allowing harm is not a legitimate method of evading responsibility for the provision of conditional basic freedoms. We must thereby turn our attention to other methods of evasion and, in turn, other morally relevant variables that help to determine whether a given situation of harm is justified or unjustified.

# 5 Knowledge and intention

Rather than simply looking at positive and negative agency, there are a variety of considerations that affect the justifiability of a given situation of harm. One such consideration is intention. If we could be said to intend that people continue to be socially deprived, our failure to help in these cases would be deemed to be all the more reprehensible. However, to reiterate one of the points from the last chapter, it would not mean that our failure to help would be suddenly transformed into *doing* something bad. That we *can* be said to intend that people continue to be socially deprived will be shown to be the case in Chapter 7. Here, the prior claim will be established that, in so far as we know what the result of a given action or inaction will be, we must intend that it comes about if we go through with it. It follows from this claim that, if we have such knowledge, the denial of intention is not a legitimate means by which to evade responsibility for a given harmful outcome.

Ambiguity surrounds the question of what we can be legitimately said to intend. This ambiguity is commonly thought to be dealt with by the doctrine of double effect. The doctrine of double effect makes a distinction between what is intended and what is foreseen and attaches moral significance to that distinction in the appraisal of harmful outcomes. It will be shown here that the distinction is often incorrectly drawn and that, when it is so drawn, the attaching of moral significance to it is evasive. Moreover, similarly to the doing/allowing distinction, even when the distinction is correctly drawn, it is not always morally significant. Given these difficulties, I will suggest that we should dispense with the doctrine. However, that doesn't mean that we should ignore the morally relevant subtleties that the doctrine of double effect is unsuccessful in articulating. They will assist us in our evaluation of how serious it is to fail to provide in the cases of social deprivation we are considering.

In the last chapter we saw with Quinn that intention can affect how we morally appraise harm. Where the resulting harm is the same, intention can make all the difference. Suppose, for example, that we are at the scene of an accident where a child has been run over. On interviewing the driver, he says he did not see the child until it was too late to stop. The child simply appeared from nowhere. In this case it would seem that we should not blame the driver for the harm caused; we might even feel sorry for him. Now let us suppose that, on interviewing the driver, we hear a different account. The driver says that, on seeing the child begin to cross the road, he changed down to third gear and accelerated. This more sinister account of events does not alter the severity of the harm inflicted on the child but it does alter how we view the situation. Our former acceptance of events, albeit with great sorrow, would be misplaced given the second account of the 'accident', due to the differences in agent intention. Similarly, on hearing that the first person at the scene of the accident failed to stop or to even call an ambulance, we might justly react differently to the explanation that they were on their way to hospital to give birth than to finding that they had a substantial life insurance policy on the child. Our moral appraisal of these examples is affected by the intention of the agent to a greater degree than it is by whether the harm came about by action or inaction. We might even find the latter instance of failing to help more morally reprehensible than the former instance of running over the child, especially if the child died through the lack of immediate medical assistance.

While the above cases are quite straightforward, many are not. Unsurprisingly, the question of whether we intend that people continue to be socially deprived is not clear cut. That we may not be deliberately setting out to harm people or to deprive them, while being important to our moral evaluation, could be deemed to be evasive. That is to say, when we build a new building that is inaccessible to some or cut welfare payments, it is arguable that we should know what the results will be and, in so far as we intend to and do build the building or cut welfare payments, we must intend and be responsible for the consequences. That does not sound like too far-fetched a claim, but in order to determine whether such an argument is coherent, we need to establish what should count as intention. That in turn requires attending to the doctrine of double effect.

The doctrine of double effect, which can be traced back at least as far as Thomas Aquinas, is based upon a distinction between what we intend as an end or a means to our end and what we foresee will come about as a result of our action or inaction. What we foresee must not be our end, nor the means to our end: it must be a 'further consequence', 'second effect' or 'side-effect'. As Quinn notes, the doctrine of double effect is typically put as a set of necessary conditions on morally permissible agency where a morally questionable bad upshot is foreseen. It requires that:

> (a) the intended final end must be good, (b) the intended means to it must be morally acceptable, (c) the foreseen bad upshot must not itself be willed (that is, it must not be, in some sense, intended), and (d) the good end must be proportionate to the bad upshot (that is, must be important enough to justify the bad upshot).[1]

Put crudely, then, the doctrine of double effect 'forbids us to produce the good by means of the bad but does not forbid us to produce it by means that also produce the bad' since it is held to be 'worse to intend to produce the bad as a means to the good than to foresee that the bad will happen as a by-product of your means to the good'.[2] Here are some examples where the doctrine of double effect is commonly held to apply. It is thought to reflect the difference between (1) a doctor giving pain-killing drugs to a patient who would otherwise die in agony, where as a side effect his death is accelerated, and a doctor giving a drug that will kill the patient as a way of preventing further pain; (2) a strategic bomber who bombs an enemy factory to destroy its productive capacity with the side effect that innocent civilians die and a terror bomber who bombs innocent civilians in order to demoralise the enemy; and (3) the removal of a pregnant mother's cancerous womb in order to save her life that has the side effect that the foetus dies and the crushing of the head of the foetus that the mother is trying to deliver in order to save the mother's life.[3]

We might similarly differentiate between cutting government spending for economic advancement with the side effect that some people are socially deprived and depriving people through benefit cuts so as to motivate them to find work. The doctrine of double effect is commonly held to permit the former act of each example and to prohibit the latter acts. However, it is questionable whether it can actually do this.

For the doctrine of double effect to be applicable, we must be able to distinguish between bad means and means that also produce the bad. Moreover, if we are to have reason to apply the doctrine, it must be shown that to intend to produce the bad as a means to the good is morally worse than to foresee that the bad will happen as a by-product of our means to the good.

Assuming that we are aiming at producing the good, it is questionable as to whether a distinction can be made between intending that the bad happen as a means to the good and foreseeing that the bad will come about as a by-product or second effect of the means to the good. One reason for this is that the required distinction is not as straightforward as the distinction between what is intended and what is purely unintentional. In my efforts to be selected for the local cricket team, for example, there is an obvious difference between me cunningly hitting you (the best batsman) over the head with my cricket bat and me, being wholly unaware that you had entered my garden, hitting you while executing a textbook fantasy cover drive. I certainly did not intend the latter but neither did I foresee it. It was purely accidental. A certain amount of opacity is generated then by the fact that foreseeing that the bad will come about as a by-product of our means to the good does not amount to the bad coming about being purely unintentional. So, if a foreseen harm cannot be equated with a purely unintentional or accidental harm, we have to look further in order to distinguish it from an intended harm.

Essential to the doctrine of double effect is the idea that what we foresee is in some way different to what we intend. Yet, given that what we foresee cannot be credibly subsumed by what is purely unintentional (that is, what is unforeseen), it is difficult to see how it can be distinguished from what we intend. If we foresee a harmful outcome resulting from our action or inaction, in what sense can we be said to not intend that it comes about if we go through with our action or inaction? The distinction, if it can be made at all, will very much depend upon what we say that we intend. And, as many writers note, this renders the distinction between intended and foreseen consequences 'excessively sensitive to redescription'.[4] Consider the example given by Foot of the fat man in the cave:

> A party of potholers have imprudently allowed the fat man to lead them as they make their way out of the cave, and he gets stuck, trapping the others behind him ... flood waters should be rising within the cave. Luckily (luckily?) the trapped party have a stick of dynamite with which they can blast the fat man out of the cave. Either they use the dynamite or they drown ... Problem: may they use the dynamite or not?[5]

Assuming that the explorers use the dynamite, there is a variety of ways in which they could describe their action. They could assert that they intended to kill the fat man so as to escape. They could say that they intended to blast a hole in the cave in order to escape, foreseeing that the fat man would die. In the style of Bennett, they could say that they intended to blow the fat man into tiny pieces for as long as it took them to escape the cave but in no way intended that he die; indeed they would have been happier if, after their escape, the fat man had reconstituted himself and sung them a song. There is a great difficulty, then, in explaining where the line is to be drawn between what our intention is and what we foresee as a further consequence. 'Since more than one thing may be strictly intended in a given choice, the pronouncements of the doctrine may depend on how the choice happens to be described.'[6]

How can we get beyond this 'embarrassing relativity'? Foot mentions the possibility of defining a criterion of 'closeness' whereby any harm that is 'very close' to our intention should count as if it were intended.[7] We might thereby consider the death of the fat man to be so closely connected with the intention to escape that it should count as if it were intended. However, while we arrive at an intuitively correct result in this example, it is unclear what should count as 'close' so as to distinguish the intended from the foreseen.

The question of what should count as close is perplexing. According to Bennett, the difficulty of explaining what closeness means gives us ample cause to abandon it as a proposal for distinguishing between what is intended and what is foreseen.[8] Similarly, Jonathan Glover asks what sort of closeness is in question:

Is it closeness in time? If so, having someone poisoned in order to prevent them catching and killing me will turn out not to be forbidden if
the poison used is very slow acting. If it is some other form of closeness,
how is it specified and what degree of it is required?[9]

It is unclear, then, as to how a particular closeness between intention and
consequence can be specified. It is also unclear as to how a concept of closeness could cope with purely unintentional or accidental outcomes. My
intention to practice my batting strokes is very close to the outcome of you
being hit by my cricket bat, even though it is completely accidental. It seems
silly to suggest that we should therefore redefine the accident. Unless the
idea of closeness is given content, then, so as to address potential difficulties, it cannot offer us a way out of our embarrassing relativity. An as yet
unspecified criterion cannot support a yet to be articulated distinction
between what is intended and what is foreseen.

The question still remains then as to how we can be said not to intend a
harm that we foresee will come about as a result of our action or inaction,
given that we go through with our action or inaction. Quinn argues that
there is one striking respect in which intending to produce the bad as a
means to the good differs from foreseeing that the bad will happen as a by-
product of our means to the good. Using example 2 stated earlier, he argues
that the terror bomber, as opposed to the strategic bomber,

> undeniably intends in the strictest sense that the civilians be involved
> in a certain explosion, which he produces, precisely because their
> involvement in it serves his goal ... his purpose requires at least this,
> that they be violently impacted by the explosion of his bombs. What
> matters is that the effect serves the agent's end precisely because it is
> an effect on civilians, [whereas the strategic bomber] can honestly
> deny that their involvement in the explosion is anything to his pur-
> pose.[10]

The difference identified here, then, is that the terror bomber 'needs the
death' of the civilians.[11] The harm itself benefits the terror bomber: it is a
'strong means' to the desired end.[12] Indeed, the terror bomber's purpose
will have been defeated if he sees that the civilians have survived; he may
drop another bomb to make sure they die but 'not so the tactical bomber'.[13]

Quinn argues that we should therefore formulate the doctrine of double
effect as distinguishing between the agency in which 'harm comes to some
victims, at least in part, from the agent's deliberately involving them in
something in order to further his purpose precisely by way of their being so
involved' (harmful direct agency) and 'harmful agency in which nothing is
in that way intended for the victims or what is so intended does not contribute to their harm' (harmful indirect agency).[14] He asserts that this shows
the genuine difference in the intentional structures of the contrasting

examples. When we intend a harm the harm contributes to our goal. A foreseen harm is nothing to our purpose.

It may very well be the case that, when we intend a harm, the harm contributes to our goal and that a foreseen harm is nothing to our purpose. (It may equally well not be.) However, it does not follow that that denotes the difference between the contrasting examples, as Quinn thinks it does. Indeed, Quinn would be wrong to say that the civilian deaths in the case of the tactical bombing are merely foreseen. Moreover, it is questionable as to whether they are nothing to the tactical bomber's purpose.

Taking example 2, the difference between what is intended and what is foreseen is said to lie in the fact that the strategic bomber would be happy if the civilians survived while the terror bomber would not be so happy. That said, however, the strategic bomber is still prepared to bomb the factory. As Bennett notes, he is prepared to manoeuvre towards death; 'he has in common with the terror bomber that he relentlessly and ingeniously pursues, for as long as he has any reason to, a path with your death on it'.[15] With both the strategic bomber and the terror bomber, then, their choice 'tips the balance'. They both consciously opt for a course leading to the victims' deaths.[16]

So, if the strategic bomber knows that the factory that he is about to bomb is full of innocent civilians, he must intend at least to drop a bomb on them if he goes through with the bombing of the factory. He may wish that they were not there and be glad if they were to survive, but this does not alter the fact that he intends to drop a bomb on them. If he sets about a course of action (or inaction) whereupon he knows that a certain harm will result, he must intend that that harm will result. If he knows that his choice will 'tip the balance', then he must intend that it does if he makes it.

Moreover, we can question whether the deaths of civilians in the case of the strategic bombing should really be called a second effect. That is to say, if the strategic bomber knows that the factory that he is about to bomb is full of innocent civilians, then he will also know that he can only destroy its productive capacity at that time by dropping a bomb on those civilians. The resulting deaths may not be the bomber's priority, but he cannot attain his goal of putting the factory out of action without those deaths. So, although there is a clear sense in which the civilian deaths *just are* a second effect of impacting the factory, there is also a sense in which the civilian deaths become an extraneous, incidental or supplementary means to the strategic bomber's end.[17]

Whether we call the strategic bomber's intention to drop a bomb on innocent civilians an intended second effect, an intended supplementary means or perhaps both is thereby open to question. We might bear that in mind when thinking about second effects that are mentioned hereafter. But, that aside, the point that is of most importance here is that the civilian deaths in both the case of the terror bomber and the strategic bomber are intended. The fact that the deaths are further removed from the aims (or stated aims) of the strategic bomber than from the aims of the terror bomber implies no lack of intention on the strategic bomber's part. Nor does it imply any necessary moral difference between the two acts.[18] Granted, we may very well want to argue in this case that the terror bomber is somehow worse, perhaps potentially more malicious, than the strategic bomber. However, it would be erroneous to contend that the latter kills only through foresight.

The difference that Quinn has identified in the above examples is not therefore between intended and foreseen harm, but between different kinds of intention. We can intend a harm as a means to our end. We can also intend a harm as a second effect of our action or inaction.

Consider example 3. The difference between the surgeon who removes the cancerous womb and the surgeon who crushes the head of the foetus is a difference in causal structure. In both cases the surgeon kills the foetus; it is just that the causal route from the movements of the surgeon to the death is longer and more complex in the case of removing the cancerous womb than in the case of crushing the head of the foetus.[19] It may be accurate to say here that the head crushing is a bad means whereas the removal of the womb is a means that also produces the bad,[20] but to assert that one case is intended and the other is foreseen is the wrong way to articulate the difference between them.

Quinn seems to be making a different distinction, then, between intending as a means and intending as a second effect. If we were to follow Quinn, the doctrine of double effect would become a distinction between what we intend as an end or a means to our end and what we intend will come about as a further effect of our action or inaction. And that distinction lacks the moral force of the distinction between intention and foresight. The above cases look a lot more like each other once we have conceded that they are all intended in one way or another. There is not, then, as clear or substantial a moral difference between different kinds of intention as there is between intention and foresight. Indeed, Quinn's formulation neglects the difference between bad outcomes that are intended and those that are genuinely foreseen. The above examples do not reflect a difference between intended and foreseen consequences. So, if the doctrine of double effect is held to make a distinction between what is intended and what is foreseen and attach moral significance to that distinction in the appraisal of harmful outcomes, it will not be relevant in distinguishing between the cases in the above examples. For the doctrine of double effect so described to be relevant, we need to amend the examples a little.

Up to now, I have suggested that if we set about a course of action whereupon we know that a harm will result, we must intend that that harm results whether it contributes to our goal or not. The only way we could be said to foresee that the harm will result, and mean something other than that we intend it to result, is if we do not know that the harm will result, that is, we are not certain. The distinction would thereby be between that which we intend to come about as an end or a means to our end and that which we foresee *might* come about as a by-product of our intended means. So, if the strategic bomber in example 2 knows that the factory he is about to bomb is full of innocent civilians, he must intend at least to drop a bomb on them if he goes through with the bombing of the factory. However, if he has notification of the production hours of the factory and bombs it outside those hours, he does not intend to inflict civilian casualties. Resulting casualties should have been foreseen, that is, the bomber must know that he could have been fed some suspect intelligence, but there is a concrete sense here in which he can be said to not have intended to inflict those casualties. Indeed, if his bombing were successful with no resulting casualties, no doubt he would be the first to say that he intended it that way.[21]

Likewise, if the doctor in example 1 gives pain killing drugs to a patient who would otherwise die in agony, knowing that the patient will certainly die as a result, he must intend that the patient dies. If, on the other hand, there is a chance that the patient will survive, the doctor will foresee that the patient may die but may very well intend that the patient survives. Unless there is a chance that the patient will survive, the doctor cannot ultimately intend anything other than that the patient dies, albeit with good pain relief, if he administers the dose. To say otherwise could simply be said to be a linguistic manoeuvre, one that can help us to avoid acknowledging the bare reality of the situation. And, while we might be more than sympathetic to such a strategy, it is not entirely honest.

Furthermore, it cannot be ruled out that we could foresee what might come about as a means to our end. For example, if you announce your arrival in my garden, I may foresee that the longer I continue to practice my fantasy batting strokes, the more likely it will be that an accident occurs. If I then continue to play my strokes regardless, I must intend to hit you. However, if you quickly sneak up behind me and I hit you thinking that you were much further away, my hitting you would not be intended (although I would be a fool if I did not foresee that it might happen). Nevertheless, I might very well end up in the team as a result.

There must, then, be some likelihood that a harm will not occur if foresight is to mean anything other than intention. The more certainty we have that a harmful outcome will result from our action or inaction, the more we can be said to intend that it come about if we go through with it. This may not work the other way; I may do $x$ because of the slim chance of $y$ happening, $y$ being what I intend. All that needs to be established, however, is that if I do $x$ and I am certain that $y$ will happen, I must intend that $y$ happen.

Through this investigation we have seen that the doctrine of double effect wrongly conflates two differences with regard to how harmful outcomes can come about. Harmful outcomes can come about through bad means and through means that also produce the bad. Harmful outcomes can also be both intended and foreseen. As a result, four possibilities can be articulated with regard to how harmful outcomes can come about. They can be intended as a means, intended as a second effect, foreseen as a means and foreseen as a second effect.[22] The doctrine of double effect is held to judge that it is worse to produce the bad as a means to the good than to foresee that the bad will happen as a second effect of your means to the good. It says nothing about harm intended as a second effect and harm foreseen as a means. We can say, then, that it is ill equipped to differentiate between the examples that it is commonly held to differentiate between, without introducing the amendments made to them. This does not imply that the original examples exhibit nothing of interest. Indeed, they exhibit subtle differences, which can be important to the moral appraisal of harmful outcomes. We should not deny that it is important that these differences are articulated. However, shoehorning them to fit the doctrine of double effect is not the answer.

That said, we can still question whether it is worse to intend that the bad happen as a means to the good than to foresee that it may come about as a second effect of our means to the good. Consider example 3 again. If it is certain that the foetus will die in both the craniotomy case and the extraction of the womb case, then, the surgeon, knowing this, must intend that the foetus die in both cases. This may sound a bit brutal and we might want to say that one option is more palatable than the other, but it does not point to the fact that the position that we have arrived at regarding intended and foreseen consequences is absurd. Rather, it points to the fact that the 'undiluted act of killing' may be morally acceptable in certain circumstances.

Jonathan Glover argues that it is hard to justify an absolute prohibition of intentional killing.[23] He cites Hart's example of a man trapped in the cabin of a blazing lorry from which it was impossible to free him. 'A bystander, in answer to his pleas, shot him and killed him to save him from further agony as he was slowly being burnt to death.'[24] We might agree that it is right here or, at least, not reprehensible for the bystander to 'aim at evil'.[25] And if the doctrine of double effect amounts to an absolute prohibition of intentional killing, then perhaps we should do without it. As Glover also argues, the undiluted act of killing can be an act of a decent and generous person.[26]

Similarly, foreseeing that the bad may come about as a by-product of our means to the good can invite greater moral condemnation than intending to produce the bad. For example, the strategic bomber, armed with information about the factory's production hours that he knows have a chance of being inaccurate, would invite greater moral condemnation if he took a chance and bombed the factory with the resulting loss of life of one innocent civilian than the terror bomber who, armed with more accurate information, bombed the factory certain of the fact that it only contained one military dictator. Now although we must be aware of the propensity for the intuitions being articulated here to be 'an artefact of the way in which the examples that trigger the intuitions are presented',[27] the fact that such intuitions can be triggered illustrates that there is more to the moral appraisal of a situation of harm than whether it comes about through intention or foresight.

Moreover, in certain cases there is nothing to choose between harm intended as a means and harm intended as a second effect, as in the case of examples 1 and 3. This does not mean that there is always nothing to differentiate between such cases. If, for example, the patient miraculously survived the dose in the second case of 1 and the doctor proceeded to 'brain him with a crowbar', we might view the cases differently. However, to deny that the doctor in the first case of 1 intends that the patient die is the wrong way to differentiate between the cases. Rather, we can identify the maliciousness of intention or the inappropriate method of treatment in the amended second case as that which sets it apart.

To summarise, as we saw much earlier with the cricketing accident, intention or lack thereof can be relevant to the moral appraisal of harm. Whether such intention manifests itself in bad means or means that also produce the bad can also be relevant although I have suggested that in many cases it is not. Where the outcome is the same, a difference in causal route is 'irrelevant to conviction'. This is not to deny, however, that maliciousness of intention can make a difference.

Furthermore, the moral appraisal of a harm that is foreseen may not be affected by the fact that it is merely foreseen. This will be explored more fully in the next chapter with regard to, for example, cases where a harm is severe or the result of negligence. I have suggested, however, that the less likely a foreseen harm is to occur, the more sympathy we might have for its perpetrator, whether it is a second effect or a means to their end. As a result, we should abandon a doctrine that misguidedly attributes a blanket moral significance to a distinction that wrongly conflates two differences with regard to how harmful outcomes come about. Such is the doctrine of double effect. It neglects the fact that there are 'numerous factors that affect the moral status of a course of conduct that has lethal consequences' and 'that they may interact in complex and perhaps as yet unidentified ways ... to determine the overall moral status of an agent's conduct'.[28] Abandoning the doctrine of double effect might enable us to pay more attention to those factors. We might look at, for example, the reasons why we can feel that some intentional killings are morally acceptable, the very reasons no doubt that have hitherto motivated us to describe such killings in a morally comforting but dishonest way.

This does not mean, however, that the notions of intended as a means, intended as a second effect, foreseen as a means and foreseen as a second effect should not be entitled to a place in our basic moral thinking.[29] On the contrary, 'it makes sense to say that a certain distinction makes a moral difference in some cases and not in others'.[30] So, while moral philosophy can dispense with the doctrine of double effect, it would be counterproductive to ignore the subtleties bound up with different productions of harmful outcomes that have come to light during the process of scrutinising it. They can and do make a moral difference.

Before we specifically apply this analysis of knowledge and intention to our cases of social deprivation, we need to consider some additional factors that often affect our moral appraisal of a situation of harm because, by implication, our investigation would be incomplete without them. The next chapter, then, looks at some other morally relevant variables that will help to determine whether our failure to provide for basic freedoms for many in our society is justified or not.

# 6  Consequences, duties and rights

So far, our investigation has suggested that there are numerous factors that affect the overall moral status of a given course of conduct. In this chapter we will look at a variety of considerations, other than positive and negative agency and intention, that affect the justifiability of a given situation of harm. These include consequence, preventability, commitments, duties and rights. I do not rank these considerations in order of importance and it must be noted that, although preventability is usually a matter of degree, zero preventability would entail that our moral judgement of a given situation of harm could not apply. It will be shown that these considerations with respect to given examples of the failure to help can be rather important.

When considering possible objections to the claim that doing is always worse than allowing, we came across the idea that harm is simply bad whether done or allowed. It may be, then, that the severity of the harm in a given situation can be the overriding factor in determining whether it is acceptable or not. Imagine, for example, that I am taking a walk by the docks of my local harbour town and I encounter a pit bull terrier that is more than a little aggressive. Luckily, there is a pallet beside me containing what look like cases of rather decent wine. I quickly pull a bottle from one of the cases and, to be sure that the dog will not bite me or anyone else, I strike it on the head. While the dog appears to be unconscious, I quickly drag it into a nearby freight container, shut the heavy air-tight iron door without a second glance and bolt it from the outside. I hear some muffled snarls as I continue on my way and, while my actions might make me unpopular with some members of animal welfare organisations, I feel that I have had a lucky escape. I may even have contributed to the continuing safety of my community.

Continuing the story, imagine that I have disappeared from the scene. Further along the waterfront, a bystander, who saw what I did earlier, encounters a man who is looking a little distraught. It turns out that he is a school teacher who has lost track of a number of his pupils. They are all here as part of their class project, which is all about the development, production, sale and delivery of precious commodities. For their case study, they have been following the journey of Veuve Clicquot, from the picking of grapes through to fermentation, bottling, storage, sale, distribution across Europe and, ultimately in this case, dispatch to Jupiter.

Now, if it turned out that the missing children happened to be in the container when I bolted it shut, it would seem that our moral appraisal of the likely disaster would not be affected by the nobility of my intention to save everyone from the dangerous dog. Indeed, nothing would seem to matter very much other than the potentially gruesome consequences. Moreover, just imagine that, having spoken with the teacher, the bystander puts two and two together. However, having considered the possibility that the children could well be trapped in the container that he saw me lock earlier, he decides not to mention it to their teacher. He does not want him to think that he is questioning his professionalism, or that he considers him to lack initiative. The bystander also decides not to return to the container and check its contents: that would take him out of his way and, in turn, make him late for a business meeting. Here, moral appraisal of the bystander's inaction, dangerous dog lovers apart, depends to a large extent upon whether the container hosts only a suffocating dangerous dog – or a suffocating dangerous dog and a party of suffocating school children. In the latter case, his inaction would be nothing short of reprehensible. The potential consequence, then, is all important in the above example and, as it increases in severity, consideration of intention or whether the harm came about by action or inaction can become relatively insignificant. Indeed, in some circumstances, such considerations may not mitigate at all.

Closely bound together with the idea that the consequence of our action or inaction can affect how we morally appraise a particular harm is the question of whether the harm is preventable. That the bystander *can* return to the container and unbolt it in the previous example is all important. Our appraisal of a particular situation of harm is bound to be affected, then, by the preventability or remediability of the situation and the ease with which the harm can be so prevented or remedied. For example, there is a sense in which there is nothing we can do when the child appears from nowhere in the road just as there is little we can do to prevent the harm caused by earthquakes even though we may be able to predict them from time to time. Our moral judgement changes in so far as we *can* stop in time to save the child that we have seen in the road or can effectively relocate people so as to save them from the effects of an impending earthquake.

The justification and acceptability of harm, whether done or allowed, can be further affected by what Bernard Williams calls our commitments.[1] There are many things including harm that we allow to happen (or do) to other people that we would make great efforts to ensure did not happen or were not done to our 'nearest and dearest'. While it could be said that all this amounts to is personal bias, there is a sense in which we feel that a particular harm is worse to us when it affects us personally. We do react differently to hearing of another death on the roads than to hearing that the death is of a person that we know and love. Likewise, the scrapping of or imposition of cuts on a particular project will affect us more if we are bound up with or committed to that particular project. While the extent to which our action or inaction should be affected by our personal commitments is questionable, it is hard to deny that it is so affected.

Consider again the Trolley Problem where there seemed to be good reason to switch the trolley from the track on which five are trapped to the track on which one is trapped. Imagine that there was a third choice, that is, another track to which we could switch where again only one person was trapped. The choice of which track to switch to would seem to be an arbitrary one, assuming that we are going to switch tracks to save the five. Now imagine that, as we are about to switch the trolley from the track with the five trapped on it, we see that the track to the left has a very close friend trapped on it. The track to the right on the other hand hosts a person unknown to us. Whether justified or not, I think that we would switch to the right-hand track. In some circumstances, we might even switch to the right-hand track if it hosted two or three or four unknown trapped people. Similarly, if the trolley was initially situated on the right-hand track, we might have no qualms about leaving it there, just as we might fail to drive to Basingstoke, for example, upon being told that a child had gone missing in that area but feel our inaction unjustified, if not inconceivable, upon being told that it was our own child that had gone missing. These examples suggest that personal commitments are morally relevant to us when evaluating a particular situation of harm and, in turn, when deciding what we should do and should not allow. From an impersonal perspective, our actions in the trolley example have no justification, especially where more than one person is trapped on the right-hand track. Similarly, the failure to drive to Basingstoke is generally held to be more acceptable when the personal element is removed.

Such considerations go some way to explain inaction in cases of profound harm from which we are to some degree detached. If, for example, our trip to an expensive restaurant entailed stepping over a group of starving Namibian refugees, I fail to see how we could continue it. Arresting television images of preventable death can be similarly conducive to changing our behaviour in as much as they bring harm quite dramatically into our sitting rooms.[2] This may point to the fact that detachment from some cases of harm in no way justifies that we do nothing about them while reinforcing the point that our personal commitments do make a difference. We would most likely be incapacitated by our emotions if we took every instance of harm personally. What we need to decide is when our distance from a given harm becomes an unjustifiable evasion of responsibility and when our commitments rightly preclude involvement.[3] We might say, for example, that mass starvation ought to command our attention while driving to Basingstoke to look for somebody else's child is not so compelling.

Personal commitments are also problematic to the extent that they conflict. That is to say, switching to the right-hand track in the trolley example will not be harmonious with the wishes of the unknown person's friend. While this is an admittedly extreme example, it is very likely that some degree of unfairness will result from personal commitments unless one is committed to impartiality. This could be as harmless as blocking somebody else's view by lifting up your child so that she can see the end of the race or ordering drinks for your friends when you know that you were not strictly next in the queue. Such inconsequential instances of bias, however, are indicative of how we might behave when life, liberty, health or security are at stake. We might countenance a similar or worse harm befalling others in the light of our commitment to saving our nearest and dearest from a particularly harmful predicament and this is bound to conflict with the interests of those others.

So, although our commitments can be relevant to our discernment of the acceptability of a situation of harm, they can conflict both with other responsibilities and with the commitments of others. It could even be said here that respect for the commitments of others may very well fall into the category of our other responsibilities. The process of deciding what our other responsibilities should be and when they should take precedence and of deciding when and how our commitments should respect the commitments of others, is the process of deciding what duties we have toward each other. Moreover, the extent to which we do respect others and have responsibilities towards them will undoubtedly affect whether harming or failing to help them is justifiable in different circumstances.

The duties that we have with regard to others provide guidelines about when irresponsibility is acceptable and when bias is unacceptable in the light of our personal commitments. Duties to act in particular ways in particular circumstances evolve from consideration of how we feel we should treat each other. For example, our desire for an extravagant meal may be tempered by the duty we feel that we have to ensure that other human beings around us are not starving to death. More mundane examples illustrate the extent to which everyday life is shaped by duties to act in particular ways. That we reprimand the naughty child, call an ambulance at the scene of an accident, help the overladen shopper off the bus, pay tax and give way at roundabouts reflects standards of behaviour we deem appropriate in given situations. Moreover, harm receives greater moral condemnation when it results from the flouting of such standards of behaviour and the corresponding duties evolving from them. The death of a child on the roads, for instance, is seen to be worse if the driver failed to stop at a pelican crossing than if the driver was observing the speed limit and the child appeared from nowhere. Though the result is the same, the neglect of the duty to drive in a safe manner contributes to how we view the situation. In this case also, our duty to drive safely overrides any personal motive we might have to not do so. That the driver may have been rushing to the bedside of her injured husband, or endeavouring to catch the last five minutes of his son's school football team debut, counts as no excuse for his or her irresponsibility.

Furthermore, when harm results from the neglect of a duty, that we see it as resulting from the neglect of a duty is more important to our moral appraisal than questions of agency. For example, the failure to call an ambulance at the scene of a serious accident is seen to be reprehensible given accepted standards of behaviour from which the duty to call the ambulance evolves, not because it is a failure to act. The moral seriousness we attach to the neglect of this duty might even entail that we deem the failure to act to be as reprehensible as if we had caused the accident. The more important a duty that is ignored, the less it matters whether the resulting harm comes about through action or inaction. We might, for example, consider the inaction of the person who lets the baby in their care slowly starve to death to be as bad as or worse than the action of the person who smothers it. The duty to care for a helpless child is the most important contribution to our moral appraisal here, over and above consideration of agency, motive or other commitments.

Duties towards people other than our nearest and dearest also evolve from the roles we assume in daily life. Roles can make all the difference when evaluating given situations of harm. For example, shooting people in the UK is not generally condoned yet we are authorised to shoot people in certain circumstances if we are part of a police armed response unit. Likewise, we saw earlier that we would feel justified in not driving to Basingstoke upon being told that a child unknown to us had gone missing. However, the situation would be altogether different if we were on call as head of a team with the specific responsibility of locating lost children. Our professional role here entails that we should make the drive. If we fail to do so, we become partly culpable for the harm befalling the lost child because of our job. Thus, the roles we have and the duties arising from them can determine whether the doing of harm or the failure to help is justified in particular situations.

We have seen, then, that duties are either laid down by general social norms as to how we should treat each other or they arise out of what is expected from particular roles. It is from these sorts of considerations that rights also evolve. Rights are inextricably bound up with duties. That is to say, rights may serve to protect duties we have to behave in particular ways and duties may result from the establishment of rights that we feel worthy of respect. For example, we may feel that the duty to feed the helpless starving child emanates from the right to life that we consider that child to have, or that the right to a fair trial emanates from the duty we feel that we have to treat people with dignity and respect. In the same way as duties, rights affect how we morally appraise particular instances of harming or failing to help. For example, if I slam the door in your face and bruise your nose, it makes a difference as to whether you are making an unwelcome attempt to enter my home, thereby violating my right to private property, or whether you are making an unwelcome attempt to enter your own home, thwarting my plans to steal your esteemed collection of Judy Garland memorabilia. Similarly, our reaction to the ambulance driver who accelerates past the scene of a terrible accident is contingent upon whether we have the right to receive medical attention and would not be so fierce in the absence of that right, especially if the ambulance belonged to a private company whose levy we had not paid.

Moreover, rights and duties are intimately bound up with what counts as harm. Our concept of harm has not remained static during the evolution of rights and duties. Nor, might we say, have rights and duties been unresponsive to changes in what we decree to be harmful. Advances in women's suffrage, for example, entail that it would now be seen as harmful to repeal the right to vote for women. The birth of the right has altered what is deemed to be acceptable political behaviour. Similarly, perception of the terrible harms endured by black people in South Africa led to a change of the political system and the advent of new rights for those people.

In addition, rights can justify actions that, in the absence of rights, could be seen to be harmful. As Quinn notes,

> Rights of competition, to give a familiar example, legitimate certain kinds of harmful positive agency – such as the shrewd but honest competition in which you take away another person's customers. The right to punish is another familiar example.[4]

We decide, then, what counts as justified and unjustified harm and this is reflected in our rights and duties. And this points to the importance of morally relevant considerations other than the doing/allowing distinction from which rights to do what could otherwise be considered harmful receive justification. Thereby, to the extent that our deliberations regarding the classification or acceptability of harm involve factors other than whether a given state of affairs was brought about or allowed to occur, our rights will not correspond emphatically with the doing/allowing distinction. Nor will the moral importance accorded to those rights.

The idea that rights and duties do not correspond with the doing/allowing distinction is opposed by Quinn. He makes a distinction between negative and positive rights:

> Negative rights are claim rights against harmful intervention, interference, assault, aggression, etc. and might therefore naturally seem to proscribe harmful positive agency, whether by action of the agent himself or by action of some object to which, by strategic inaction, he lends a hand. Positive rights, on the other hand, are claim rights to aid or support, and would therefore seem to proscribe harmful negative agency.[5]

Quinn argues that Foot's idea that general negative rights are, *ceteris paribus*, harder to override than general positive rights is intuitively correct. He argues that negative rights 'define the terms of moral possibility' and that their precedence is essential to the moral fact of our lives, minds, and bodies really being ours. What this amounts to is the claim that rights not to be harmed by action or intentional inaction should take precedence over rights to be helped. Rights to punish or economically destroy others, for example, are anomalies that oppose Quinn's doctrine in particular cases but that he argues do not require that it be qualified. What I have been suggesting throughout this section is that such anomalies, along with others, point to the fact that the evaluation of harm is much more complicated than assessing whether it came about through action or inaction. That being so, the evaluation of the importance of rights cannot rest on an assessment as to whether they are rights not to be harmed or to be helped without suffering the same pitfalls.

We saw earlier that Quinn coped with problematic cases of intentional allowing of harm by making the unusual assertion that they count as cases of doing. This is reflected in his definition of negative rights whereby we have a right against 'strategic inaction'. The problems with Quinn's position cited earlier can be applied to his definition of rights and his assertion that negative rights take precedence over positive rights. Just as we saw that negative agency can be unjustifiable in some cases and that some cases of positive agency can be justified, we can argue here that some instances of the violation of positive rights can be unjustifiable and some violations of negative rights justified. We can further argue that Quinn's position is not saved by the proviso that the intentional violation of a positive right counts as the violation of a negative right. This is because there are other morally relevant variables that help to determine whether a situation of harm is justified or unjustified and these are bound to help to determine whether the violation of a right, whether negative or positive, is justified or not. Indeed, discussion as to whether a right can be justifiably violated cannot directly correlate with Quinn's moral emphasis on the distinction between negative and positive agency in cases of harm because, as we have seen, *rights themselves* affect the moral appraisal of negative and positive agency in cases of harm. So, in the same way that the justification of harm rests on more than whether it came about through action or inaction, the justification of the violation of rights will rest on more than whether it is a right against harmful action or a right against harmful inaction. It will not simply follow that rights not to be harmed are more important than rights to help.

The distinction, then, between negative and positive rights and a thesis of precedence based on the distinction between doing and allowing harm is necessarily incomplete due to the omissions and shortcomings of the distinction on which it is based. It is more fitting to suggest that some rights will take precedence in virtue of what they protect or secure and in what circumstances, just as the reprehensibility of agency depends on what is jeopardised or neglected and in what circumstances. Moreover, it is harder to make a distinction between negative and positive rights than it is to make a distinction between negative and positive agency. Whereas there is a clear sense in which doing something is different to not doing something, it is less clear how a right against something can be differentiated from a right to something. We saw in the discussion about freedom that there was no special positive freedom *to* that was not also a negative freedom *from*. Negative and positive rights can be seen to be logically linked in the same way. For example, the negative right against interference can be seen to imply the positive right to that which we would not want to be interfered with and vice versa. At the very least, the enjoyment of negative rights is dependent on the positive right to life of the helpless infant. Given this we might say, contra Quinn, that both negative and positive rights 'define the terms of moral possibility' and that certain positive rights are required to ensure that 'your life is yours'.[6]

We have seen, then, that rights, in a similar way to duties, can affect both the moral appraisal of harm and what counts as harm in a way that can transcend the doing/allowing distinction. Furthermore, we have seen that the moral importance accorded to rights and thus the moral reprehensibility of their violation in particular situations is not consistent with the moral emphasis on the distinction between harming and failing to help. Rights upset the moral emphasis on the distinction between harming and failing to help in so far as they are morally relevant variables that affect the appraisal of a situation of harm. They, along with consideration of knowledge and intention, consequence, preventability, commitments and duties, help to determine whether the doing or allowing of harm is justified in given situations.

The preoccupation of this section with the nature and moral relevance of the distinction between harming and failing to help evolved from the requirement that society would have to make provisions to secure freedom for those who find themselves deprived in one way or another. Through investigating how serious it can be to fail to help, we have discerned that allowing harm is not always more acceptable than doing it. However, that we have had to investigate whether failing to help can be as bad or worse than harming admits to a certain extent that harming is usually worse than failing to help, all other things being equal. We might say, for example, that the failure to free my wealthy uncle from the wardrobe that he has inadvertently locked himself into when I know that he is frail and that I am the sole beneficiary of his will is more morally reprehensible than my administering him a lethal injection when he has pleaded with me to end his terminal suffering. However, we would think it worse still if I opened the wardrobe door in the former situation and then proceeded to shoot my uncle, knock him down the stairs or push him through a first floor window. To this extent, then, the doing of harm can be seen to be more morally reprehensible than allowing it to happen in the same circumstances. As

Kagan notes, in the case of doing harm, 'the good that the victim has, eg, his life, is one that he has and can maintain independently of the agent' whereas, in the case of allowing harm, 'the very fact that aid from the agent is required by the victim brings out the fact that the good in question is not one that is independent of the agent'.[7] Kagan argues that this may provide a key to the offensiveness of doing harm. Put crudely, when we kill an agent, they would not have otherwise died but, when we fail to save an agent, they would have died anyway.

Although this may be the source of our attaching significance to the difference between doing and allowing, it does not permit us to infer that taking away freedom is always worse than failing to provide for it. It might permit us to contend that given the exact same circumstances, taking away a particular freedom is morally worse than failing to provide for it, but that does not get us very far at all. It certainly does not entail that failing to provide for freedom has no moral importance and so cannot go so far as to serve as a justification for the continuing failure to provide in our cases of deprivation. Moreover, we have seen both from the above discussion and from consideration of the doctrine of double effect, that there is more to our moral evaluation than simply the question of whether we are harming or failing to help. So, just as harm cannot be justified solely by reference to its not being the result of positive agency, unfreedom cannot be justified solely by the claim that it has not been imposed.

That securing freedom for those who find themselves deprived involves provision, and, thus, that the failure to secure such freedom falls into the category of failing to help, does not therefore signal an end to the debate. It does not amount to enough to deny that we be morally obligated to make such provision. Even if we grant that the doing of a harm is worse than the allowing of the same harm in the same circumstances, we have seen that, in different circumstances, allowing a harm to occur can be just as bad or worse than doing the same harm. We have also seen that all sorts of things can contribute to those circumstances. The importance of other factors with respect to our moral appraisal of a given situation of harm should therefore be conceded. By implication, we must also establish how those morally relevant variables specifically apply to our different cases of social deprivation, so as to discover whether the continued failure to help in those cases can be justified.

# 7 Applications

In this chapter, we will see how consideration of knowledge and intention, consequence, remediability, commitments, duties and rights specifically affects our evaluation of the failure to provide in the case of relative social deprivation and, more specifically, socially induced disability. As a result of the application of those factors, the methods of evasion hitherto discussed will be shown to fail. Indeed, it will be shown that all of the above factors contribute to our classifying the failure to provide in cases of social deprivation as morally reprehensible. That failure remains unjustified.

We have seen that intention can make all the difference to the moral appraisal of a situation of harm. I suggested in Chapter 5 that the only credible way in which we can be said to foresee that a harm will result and mean something other than that we intend it to result is if we are not certain that that harm will result. The ramifications of this with regard to social deprivation are interesting. That is to say, although it would be difficult to contend that we had set out to curtail the freedom of people who are disabled and deprived, that we continue to fail to provide as a society, given knowledge of the consequences, is a different story.

Taking the social aspect of disability first, it would be difficult to contend that the lack of freedom experienced by people is the result of anyone's malicious intention. Discrimination against people with impairments in the labour market may be said to be intentional in some cases, but it can often be the result of ignorance. Similarly, it is unlikely that the effects of segregated mainstream education upon people with impairments have at the outset been maliciously intended and it would be outrageous if they were. It is more likely that there has been little informed thought about it, not that that serves as any excuse for the deprivations bound up with such a policy. Indeed, the fact that little attention is paid to the needs of people with impairments might go some way to explain the inadequacies of welfare measures, health and social support services and the physical environment. We have shown less than a little foresight.

Likewise, it would be difficult to contend that the limitation of freedom for those who are more generally relatively deprived is the result of malicious intention. It is unlikely that governments set out to create a homelessness problem, to ensure that welfare payments are hopelessly inadequate or to build housing estates that demean their inhabitants. The effects of government measures may in some cases have been foreseen, but it is likely that the intended consequences were somewhere near their opposite.

However, it is increasingly hard to deny that we know what many of the effects of our inaction will be with regard to cases of social deprivation. We can be certain that, if we continue to fail to provide in these cases, people will continue to be confined to the margins of society. We also know that if we make provision in these cases, we will be facilitating the enjoyment of conditional basic freedoms. I suggested in Chapter 5 that the more certainty we have that a harmful outcome will result from our action or inaction, the more we can be said to intend that it comes about if we go through with our action or inaction. Now it may sound odd to attribute intention to a collectivity such as society, even though a particular majority at a particular time elect representatives on the basis of what they intend to do. However, it sounds a lot less odd to attribute intention to something like a government or a cabinet. Indeed, prospective governments publish manifestos that are full of promises and intentions. And, however fragmented, confused or insincere their approach turns out to be, to the extent that we hold governments responsible we can be said to ascribe intentions to them too.

At the very least, then, there is a sense in which we can be said to hold governments responsible for implementing social and economic policies, with intent, on the basis of what they promised and were elected to do. Moreover, a government tends to be the only unit that *can* direct and coordinate social and economic policy across a given jurisdiction. With that in mind, along with a modest estimation of the knowledge that governments are likely to have with respect to social problems and needs, we can argue that for a government to cite lack of intention with regard to the continuation of unfreedom in cases of social deprivation is not a legitimate move. It is not a legitimate method of evading responsibility for continued inaction. Indeed, we can assert here that to continue to fail to provide in cases of social deprivation, when a government is certain that people will remain unfree as a result, is to intend that they remain unfree. This, in turn, has ramifications with regard to the legitimacy of an appeal to the doing/allowing distinction. A government will know what the result of its inaction will be and so it must intend that that result comes about if it continues not to act. This may not amount to malicious intention. A government may not intend at all that people remain unfree as a means to an end, like low taxes. However, at the very least, it must intend that people remain unfree as a second effect of its failure to act. It might even be said that we as citizens become complicit with such a state of affairs in as much as we do not encourage or vote for a change in outlook and policy. Moreover, even if it were contended (by some stretch of the imagination) that a government cannot be certain that its failure to act will result in continued unfreedom, it would not escape moral culpability. This is due to both the strong likelihood of the foreseen harm occurring and the profundity of that harm.

So, ignorance can no longer serve as an excuse in cases of social deprivation. Furthermore, as just mentioned, our knowledge here is not of a futile consequence. As we have seen, the severity of a given harm makes an important contribution to our moral evaluation of it. The severity of the harm in more serious cases of relative social deprivation is profound, as it is also in cases of socially induced disability. Indeed, it has been shown that both relative social deprivation and socially induced disability are tantamount to unfreedom and that the freedoms at stake are important basic freedoms upon which the enjoyment of other valuable or more superficial freedoms is conditional. Although it is rarely a matter of life and death (unlike the examples referred to in preceding sections) relative social deprivation and socially induced disability do restrict participation in the kinds of activities that we deem to be valuable. And the deprivation of those freedoms to participate must be morally serious in as much as it is the deprivation of a valued way of life. Remonstration against harmful action or inaction would have no basis unless we thought there was something worth protecting or facilitating – and the freedom to participate in the activities that we value is a good candidate for that something. Given this, we have a strong case for arguing that the harm entailed by the limitation of freedom of people who are relatively socially deprived (with regard to habitation, employment, access to services and social interaction) and of people with impairments (with regard to education, employment, travel, leisure and social interaction) is very serious and should factor heavily in our moral evaluation. That the problems we are considering are the result of negative agency in most cases is rendered less important due to the profundity of those problems.

Our moral appraisal must be further affected by the fact that in the cases of social deprivation so described, the harm is to a large extent preventable or remediable. The concerns of this section were born from the requirement that something needs to be provided, both in the general case of relative social deprivation and the more specific one of socially induced disablility. This is indicative of the fact that something can be provided in these cases, to alleviate or eradicate restrictions on freedom. In all but a few cases freedom can be facilitated, whether through the removal of obstacles or through some sort of provision. We can, for example, cease to segregate schools and discriminate against people with impairments in the workplace. Likewise, we can make the physical environment more aesthetically palatable to all and more accessible to people who use wheelchairs. Moreover, benefits and support services could be made adequate and stigmatisation could be tackled with respect to both people with impairments and people who are more generally relatively deprived. Such changes could be easily made and, although they would involve substantial cost, facilitation of the enjoyment of conditional basic freedoms is a massive benefit. So, that we are able to make society more tolerant of and sympathetic to the needs of all the people who are a part of it should affect the moral appraisal of our doing nothing to our detriment.

Might the moral appraisal of our failure to provide in different cases of social deprivation be affected by the notion of personal commitments? This very much depends upon what they are although, at the very least, people living in the UK cannot escape the fact that the hardships being discussed are being endured in their country. Thus, we are not detached from them to the same extent as we tend to feel we are from harmful situations occurring on the other side of the world. Moreover, provision in the cases of relative social deprivation and socially induced disability would neither require the abandoning of our personal commitments nor their curtailment to any significant degree, assuming that we are not personally committed to oppressing people who find themselves socially deprived. Indeed, provision would be harmonious with the commitments of many. Provision would obviously assist people who are relatively deprived in attending to their identity-conferring commitments. So might it relieve the financial or spatial burdens of those close to them if they are in any position to help. Furthermore, the disadvantages suffered by people with impairments are alleviated to a great extent by the informal help of family and friends. Those who assist and empower people with impairments are close to a situation that they consider to be unacceptable. Provision to secure basic freedoms would thus have a positive impact on those people as well as on people with impairments themselves.

Furthermore, we have seen that the situations of hardship in question are neither isolated nor unimportant. As a result, even if we felt detached from them, our keeping a distance from those situations could be seen to be an unjustifiable evasion of responsibility. We would have only to consider the bizarre evolutionary twist described in Chapter 2, or to think of our own son or daughter being homeless, receiving an inadequate education, not being able to get a job or simply not being able to visit us, to recognise that there is more to people's commitments in cases of social deprivation than the sort of personal bias that makes us jump the queue at a bar. That both relative social deprivation and socially induced disability are issues of social justice, then, adds to the force of the argument that we should not keep our distance from them.[1]

Although many people do not need to, putting ourselves in the position of someone who is socially deprived in one way or another, or the position of someone who is close to a person who is socially deprived, can elicit what *we* would expect in that position. Consideration as to how we would feel that we should be treated or how we would feel that those close to us should be treated in a given situation is indicative of how we should treat others, assuming we want to be consistent. In this sense, we call the ambulance at the scene of a serious accident because we would want somebody to do the same if it was us that had had the accident and we give way at roundabouts because we expect that others will do so in the same circumstances. In the same sense, we can argue that people without impairments should support provision in the case of socially induced disability because, if it was they who were impaired, they would not expect their impairment to entail a loss or limitation of freedom to take part in everyday life due to economic, political, social, legal, environmental and interpersonal constraints and, more than likely, they would be outraged if it did.[2] Likewise, we can argue that people who are not relatively deprived in the more general sense should support provision in the case of relative social deprivation because they would consider it to be indecent if *they* were without the security and resources that relatively deprived people often go without. And from this line of argument it can be asserted that we have a duty to provide both for people with impairments and for people who are more generally socially deprived. At the very least, I think we would hope that, if we found ourselves in any such circumstances, they would not bring with them such a loss of freedom. To this extent, we can infer that we ought to assume a duty to provide in these cases of social deprivation.

Another way of arguing that we have a duty to provide in cases of social deprivation is by inference from other duties to provide. Consider, for example, the case of the person who lets the helpless child in their care slowly starve to death. Our duty to care for the helpless child in this case might evolve from the biological fact of our being its mother or father. So, imagine instead that the person in question is not related to the child in their care – the child's entire family have perished in a boating accident. I think that we would say that the person still has a duty to care for the helpless child, or at least to find somebody who will, because they are the only one knowingly in a position to keep the child alive. We can argue from this that, given the scale of provision required in our different cases of social deprivation, the government knows that, unless it collectively makes provisions to secure freedom for people, nobody else will and quite radical inequalities of basic human freedoms will continue to exist. Moreover, given the value we place on our freedoms and, especially, the value of the conditional basic freedoms at stake in different cases of social deprivation, we can strongly argue that the government has a duty to make provision in these cases.

Since we have seen that harm receives greater moral condemnation when it results from the neglect of a duty, that we may have a duty to liberate people who find themselves socially deprived in one way or another contributes to the moral seriousness of our failure to provide. Having said this, the concerns of this investigation partly evolved from the fact that it would seem that governments now do not feel that they have a duty to sufficiently provide for people who encounter social deprivations of a remediable kind. It might therefore be said to be unfair to assert that the failure to provide in cases of social deprivation is to neglect duties or to infringe upon rights since they are hitherto unknown and not argued for. The point is, however, that, given the results of our investigation so far, it is clear that we *should* assume a duty to make provisions so as to ensure that people with impairments and people who are relatively deprived more generally can enjoy the important basic freedoms that they are presently to a large extent denied.

We might argue further that people with impairments and people who are relatively deprived more generally should have a right to important basic freedoms. Indeed, unless we actually differentiate between different sorts of people, or we deny that people who are not socially deprived in the different sorts of ways we have looked at feel that they have a right to certain basic freedoms, to withhold that right from people who are deprived is more than a little inconsistent. It is hard to deny that people who do not find themselves socially deprived in the UK feel that they have a right to certain basic freedoms, since the fact that they do set the parameters from which we discerned the disadvantages bound up with social deprivation. Indeed, what we take for granted in terms of rights and freedoms both helps to define what we consider to be deprivation and generates our concern about it. Similarly, we do not officially demarcate between different people and assign rights accordingly. Moreover, we might ask what criteria could be used to justifiably do so. To deny the right to important basic freedoms to a person because they cannot read, run, hear, add up, stand up or afford to pay rent is as arbitrary as denying the same right on the grounds of hair or skin colour, lack of strength or because a person cannot sing. As we have seen also, the fact that such rights may be positive rights requiring positive measures need not entail that they are unimportant or that their violation is less serious than that of negative rights. So, although it would be unfair to contend that we are presently neglecting duties and violating rights, the fact that there are strong arguments in support of assuming those duties and assigning those rights to everyone in our community should affect the moral evaluation of our failure to provide in present cases of social deprivation. This is important in so far as it differentiates between the failure to provide in those cases and, for example, the failure to provide for the freedom to drink fine wine on Jupiter, which is something that we similarly do not have a right to, but is also something that we do not feel that we should have a right to.

Having looked at how the variables that affect our moral appraisal of harm specifically apply both to the general case of relative social deprivation and to socially induced disability, we should be able to evaluate whether the failure to provide in these cases is justified or not. We have seen that, in most cases, we are not doing harm and that to secure freedom for people requires considerable social provision. However, we have knowledge of the harmful effects of our failure to provide in these cases and these effects have been articulated as limitations to the realisation of important basic freedoms. In so far as we have that knowledge, we can be said to intend that these situations continue if we continue to do nothing about them. Furthermore, the situations so described are, in the main, utterly remediable. We can make provision to ensure that everyone in our community can both possess and realise the very basic freedoms upon which participation in so many activities is conditional. This would not require that our personal commitments be curtailed to any significant degree and, even if it did, the severity of the hardships in question here demands that they should be so curtailed. Having said this, our failure to provide for people who are presently socially deprived cannot be said to be the neglect of an established duty or the violation of an established right, although there are strong arguments to suggest that we should assume a duty to provide in these cases and that people should be assigned rights to important basic freedoms. This would help to make sure that people with and without impairments, who might currently wind up having to endure a raft of social deprivations, do not continue to do so.

Given the above, we can assert that consideration of agency is outweighed by the application of other morally relevant factors to cases of social deprivation when it comes to our moral appraisal of the harm. That is to say, our failure to rectify the situation of harm in these cases cannot be justified by reference to its not being maliciously inflicted given the significance of other considerations. Therefore, recourse to the doing/allowing distinction is not a legitimate method of evading responsibility for the provision of important basic freedoms. It doesn't get us off the moral hook. Indeed, reasons to help outweigh excuses not to and so, in as much as we have responsibilities with regard to others in our community, feel compassionately towards them and value the basic freedoms that we take for granted, provision to secure those basic freedoms should take a high priority. Consideration of our knowledge, the consequences and the remediability of the social deprivations described serves to classify our inaction as both theoretically unjustified and morally reprehensible.

If we felt justified in failing to help in the light of these considerations, we might also feel justified in failing to call the ambulance, failing to divert the trolley, stepping over the Namibian refugees or letting the helpless child starve. Although, as I pointed out earlier, our inaction does not typically result in death in these cases, the analogy holds because death is not a prerequisite for moral condemnation. For example, we would still condemn the person who let the helpless child starve to the brink of death and then gave her a turkey twizzler. In a similar sense we can condemn the failure to alleviate the deprivation of conditional basic freedom. Moreover, although our inaction in these cases is not the neglect of an established duty as perhaps it is in the other cases, the reasons why we have a duty in the other cases, apart from the saving of life in itself, constitute the reasons to liberate in the less severe cases. That is, we tend to save, respect and nurture life because we consider it to have enormous quality and potential. It is valuable and precious. So, to then be unconcerned with what that quality is, whether that potential is realised and, more specifically, the impact that social deprivation can have on people's lives amounts to being unconcerned with what we tend to save life *for*. In this way, if we care little about human freedom and the impact that limitations of freedom can have on quality of life, it is far from obvious why we should care very much about saving life itself.

It has been shown, then, that we cannot retain the same moral emphasis on the distinction between harming and failing to help and that the failure to provide in our cases of social deprivation is morally serious. Our failure to provide thereby remains unjustified. We would have either to deny that basic freedoms are important or classify the moral worth of people, in view of, for example, their functional capacities, business acumen or simply how lucky they happen to have been, so as to legitimately exclude certain sections of our community from receiving adequate social provision. Then we might be justified in failing to liberate in cases of social deprivation. However, in so far as we do not do either of these things and, more to the point, do not want to, we should be obligated to provide in cases of both relative social deprivation and socially induced disability.

# 8 Nozick's retort
## Natural assets and arbitrariness

Other than through recourse to the distinction between harming and failing to help or the doctrine of double effect, another way of avoiding responsibility with regard to social deprivation could be to argue that it is simply hard luck to be socially deprived and that this in no way requires anything of those who happen to be lucky. Business acumen and functional capacity might be more important in determining the sort of life that we are likely to have than was previously envisaged as fair. Indeed, Robert Nozick argues that, although it is a matter of luck, people are entitled to their natural assets and to what flows from them. The emphasis switches here from the plight of the badly off to the rights of the better off. The idea is that self-owners are not obliged to help others and should not be forced to do so. If this idea is compelling, we might be justified in continuing to fail to provide for freedom in cases of relative social deprivation and socially induced disability. I will argue that it is not.

The question as to what effects morally arbitrary factors should have on individual life chances is a contentious one in political theory. Rawls argues, for example, that we should not eliminate the natural distinctions between persons but, as we have seen, we should employ them to the benefit of the worst off. This idea is subject to intuitively appealing criticism by Nozick. In this section I will look at Nozick's position and explore the idea of what a natural asset actually is. I will suggest both that the arguments for his position are far from convincing and that the whole idea of natural assets is conceptually problematic. Rather than basing a theory upon the idea that some natural differences are inherently fortuitous or problematic, I will argue that there is a prior need to challenge the particular social system from which such categorisations evolve.

It is inevitable that people are different. The problem that liberal theories of justice attempt to deal with is that, left to their own devices in the free market, people will exploit those differences to their own advantage. Some will enjoy advantages over others, then, as a result of their natural differences. The problem is that in no way can the fortuitously talented or the arbitrarily disadvantaged be said to deserve their talents or handicaps; the advantages that some enjoy over others are the results of natural or historical accidents and so are therefore morally arbitrary. The argument continues that, since nobody deserves their place in the natural lottery, the talented do not deserve, in any moral sense, what flows from the exercise of their talents. So, it would be unfair to let people exploit their talents at the expense of others. For Rawls, such unfairness constitutes an objection to a system of natural liberty, whereby:

> The existing distribution of income and wealth, say, is the cumulative effect of prior distributions of natural assets — that is, natural talents and abilities – as these have been developed or left unrealised, and their use favoured or disfavoured over time by social circumstances and such chance contingencies as accident and good fortune. Intuitively, the most obvious injustice of the system of natural liberty is that it permits distributive shares to be improperly influenced by these factors so arbitrary from a moral point of view.[1]

Should we therefore eliminate the natural differences between people? Doing that would likely entail a severe curtailment of the freedom of people to exercise their natural features and would thus be highly problematic. Rawls has another way of dealing with the morally arbitrary natural differences between people, which is manifest in his articulation of the difference principle:

> We see then that the difference principle represents, in effect, an agreement to regard the distribution of natural talents as a common asset and to share in the benefits of this distribution whatever it turns out to be. Those who have been favoured by nature, whoever they are, may gain from their good fortune only on terms that improve the situation of those who have lost out ... No one deserves his greater natural capacity nor merits a more favourable starting place in society. But it does not follow that one should eliminate these distinctions. There is another way to deal with them. The basic structure can be arranged so that these contingencies work for the good of the least fortunate.[2]

Thus, Rawls argues that we should be allowed to exploit our natural differences but that this should only be done if it benefits the least fortunate. However, it is far from obvious that this should be so. For example, Sandel argues that if the arbitrariness of my talents makes them ineligible to serve my ends, 'there seems no obvious reason why their arbitrariness within any particular society should not make them ineligible to serve that society's ends as well'.[3] Nozick also has reservations with regard to Rawls' difference principle, asking:

> If people's assets and talents couldn't be harnessed to serve others, would something be done to remove these exceptional assets and talents, or to forbid them from being exercised for the person's own benefit or that of someone else he chose, even though this limitation

wouldn't improve the absolute position of those somehow unable to harness the talents and abilities of others for their own benefit?[4]

Nozick objects to the view that we should not be allowed to exploit our natural differences since they are morally arbitrary. He does not assert, however, that natural differences between people are not morally arbitrary, or that our criterion for moral arbitrariness is itself arbitrary. Rather, he asserts that 'Whether or not people's natural assets are arbitrary from a moral point of view, they are entitled to them, and to what flows from them.'[5] Contra Rawls, Nozick asks, 'Why shouldn't holdings partially depend upon natural endowments? (They will also depend on how these are developed and on the uses to which they are put).'[6] He charges Rawls with assuming that equality is the natural state of affairs, the starting point from which any departures require stringent justification. This assumption of equality as a norm can be questioned, according to Nozick:

> Why ought people's holdings to be equal, in the absence of special moral reason to deviate from equality? Why is equality the rest position of the system, deviation from which may be caused only by moral forces? Many 'arguments' for equality merely assert that differences between persons are arbitrary and must be justified ... Why must differences between persons be justified? Why think that we must change, or remedy, or compensate for any inequality which can be changed, remedied, or compensated for? ... The legitimacy of altering social institutions to achieve greater equality of material condition is, though often assumed, rarely argued for.[7]

Nozick certainly does not argue for the legitimacy of altering social institutions to achieve greater equality of material condition. Rather, he presents the counter-argument that people are entitled to their natural assets even if it is not the case that they can be said to deserve them. Nozick's use of the notion of entitlement is an attempt to avoid the problem of trying to argue that we *can* be said to deserve the outcome of natural or historical accident.[8] His argument runs as follows:

1. People are entitled to their natural assets.
2. If people are entitled to something, they are entitled to whatever flows from it (via specified types of processes).
3. People's holdings flow from their natural assets.
4. Therefore, people are entitled to their holdings.
5. If people are entitled to something, then they ought to have it (and this overrides any presumption of equality there may be about holdings).[9]

This argument is wholly opposed to the Rawlsian notion of regarding the distribution of natural talents as a common asset. Nozick regards such a notion as open to the charge that it fails to take seriously the distinction between persons. It is a condition of us properly owning ourselves that we are entitled to what flows from the exercise of our natural talents. Furthermore, he argues that there is no need to regard the distribution of natural talents as a common asset since people's talents and abilities are an asset to a free community. Therefore, not only does Rawls' difference principle violate people's entitlements to the holdings that flow from their natural assets, it also does not constitute a criticism of a free society, since:

> In a free society, people's talents do benefit others, and not only themselves ... others in the community benefit from their presence and are better off because they are there rather than elsewhere or nowhere. Life, over time, is not a constant sum game, wherein if greater ability or effort leads to some getting more, that means that others must lose.[10]

How might we respond to this? Not only does this argument support the moral emphasis on the distinction between harming and failing to help, it emphasises the benefits of failing to help or, at least, the benefits of not forcing others to help. Closer scrutiny of Nozick's 'acceptable argument' may enable us to challenge it. Clause 2 of Nozick's argument contains the condition 'via specified types of processes' and, as we will see, clause 3 gives us a good impression of what Nozick thinks they will and will not entail. However, it is safe to assume that he would *not* hold us to be entitled to whatever flows from our native endowments if such entitlement violated the liberty of others. And the main point here is that clause 2 gives us the theoretical room to slot in and argue for a variety of different specified types of processes, including ones that are different to those that Nozick envisages. In principle, there is nothing to stop us from regarding a strong egalitarian distributive scheme as a favoured specified type of process. At the very least, Nozick gives us no reason to have to rule out some sort of redistributive scheme as a legitimate process that might limit what people are entitled to as a result of the exercise of their natural assets.

However, the third clause that 'people's holdings flow from their natural assets' certainly suggests that Nozick's idea of the correct specified process will not disrupt such a flow. He rules out the possibility that a specified type of process might stipulate for reasons other than safeguarding liberty (or for reasons that safeguard a different conception of liberty to Nozick's) that people are not entitled to the holdings that flow from their natural assets. Yet entertaining such a possibility is perfectly sensible. We might argue that, for example, even though people are entitled to their natural talents and to quite a lot that flows from them, they may not be entitled to *all* the holdings that flow from them. Indeed, just as we saw when considering the doctrine of doing and allowing that there are strong reasons to provide in cases of social deprivation, there are corresponding reasons as to why we should not be entitled to all holdings that flow from our natural talents. We should give some of them up so as to provide important basic freedoms for others. If, then, it is legitimate to suggest that we should not be entitled to *whatever* flows from the exercise of our natural talents, we can challenge both the second clause of Nozick's argument and the inference from clause 3 to clause 4.

Moreover, the third clause of Nozick's argument can only hold in a particular social set up. Unsurprisingly, the clause that people's holdings flow from their natural assets need only be true within a free market economy and minimal state. Other systems might specify different rules with regard to the flow of holdings and the possibility of other legitimate systems renders clause 3 incomplete.

The idea that it is legitimate to suggest and defend alternative specified types of processes with respect to Nozick's scheme is reinforced by Rawls, who does precisely that. The condition placed on clause 2 by Nozick allows Rawls to superimpose his own idea of a specified type of process. He remoulds Nozick's argument as follows:

1. People are entitled to their native endowments: that is, our native endowments belong to us and the integrity of the person is protected by the basic rights included under the first principle of justice.
2. If people are entitled to something, they are entitled to what flows from it via a process that is fair; and so in the case of the basic structure, via a process of pure adjusted procedural justice regulated by the two principles of justice with the difference principle. (This is the specified kind of process appropriate for the case of the basic structure.)
3. People's holdings flow in part from their native endowments. (The institutional background and the system of social cooperation also affects our holdings).
4. Therefore, people are entitled to their holdings, that is, to what they may legitimately expect from the use to which they have put their skills and talents within the existing institutional background (as regulated by the two principles of justice).
5. If people are entitled to something, then they ought to have it (and this overrides any presumption of equality not expressed by the difference principle and the prior principles of justice).[11]

Rawls further argues, in response to Nozick's charge that the difference principle fails to take seriously the distinction between persons, that what is regarded as a common asset is the distribution of native endowments, not our native endowments themselves:

> the question of the ownership of our endowments does not arise ... it is persons themselves that own their endowments: the psychological and physical integrity of persons is guaranteed by the basic rights and liberties that fall under the first principle of justice.[12]

Whether the above is an adequate response to Nozick's charge about the distinction between persons is questionable. But, that aside, Rawls has cleverly deposited his notion of justice as fairness in Nozick's argument as a specified type of process. However, Nozick need not tuck his bat under his arm and head for the pavilion just yet: the intuitively appealing questions that he aims at Rawls' difference principle still apply. Nozick and Rawls simply disagree on what amounts to a fair procedure in deciding what people's entitlements flowing from their natural assets should be. Nozick can allow Rawls' adjustment of the second clause of his argument to read 'If people are entitled to something they are entitled to what flows from it via a procedure that is fair'; it is just that he holds Rawls' specified process to be anything but fair to the talented. Nozick could exclude Rawls from playing his game altogether if he dropped the condition to clause 2 but, although doing this would rule out the possibility of welfare measures, it would rule in market anarchy at the possible expense of freedom. Even Nozick, it seems, would not want to take that step. Thus, given that, as we have seen, it is legitimate and compelling to suggest alternatives to Nozick's scheme that disrupt the flow of people's holdings from their natural talents, if only a little, Nozick's conclusion that 'whether or not people's assets are arbitrary from a moral point of view, they are entitled to them, and to what flows from them', need not be accepted. Indeed, whatever we may think of some of Nozick's criticisms of Rawls, the strong arguments in support of social provision in cases of social deprivation suggest that we should not accept his conclusion.

So far, we have seen that Nozick's own position is far from convincing due to the dubious nature of the claim that, if people are entitled to something, they are entitled to whatever flows from it and the falsity of the claim that people's holdings flow from their natural assets for any system other than a free market. Even though we have reason to believe that Nozick's conclusion with regard to entitlement of holdings flowing from morally arbitrary natural assets is already problematic, we can delve deeper and investigate just what natural assets are taken to be. If the very idea of natural assets can be seen to be dubious, so presumably can a theory of entitlement that hinges on their exercise.

A question worth asking here is whether there really are natural inequalities between people, and if there are, whether the social inequalities that they lead to are inevitable. If there are such things as natural assets and advantages then, by implication, there must be natural handicaps and disadvantages also. This entails that there are natural inequalities between those who are naturally advantaged and those who are naturally disadvantaged. However, as was noted in Chapter 3, there is a difficulty with exactly what one would wish to call a natural advantage, disadvantage or inequality. As Kymlicka points out, 'it is impossible to determine ... what counts as a natural advantage. That depends on what sort of skills people value'.[13] For example, many artists and musicians go unrecognised. Even though they have what many would consider to be immense natural talent or ability, it may lead to no advantage whatsoever. And, even if they do gain recognition, that will not necessarily convert into financial success or other kinds of advantage. For others, of course, recognition does lead to considerable financial success: their talent becomes an asset. However, the correlation between talent and financial success is rarely obvious or consistent, which lends support to the suggestion that there is at least some social influence upon how talents are rewarded, if not defined (as we will see shortly).

Moreover, a 'natural' asset can at the same time be an asset in one place yet not in another. It can also be specific to a particular age or era. With respect to the former, the varied reception of the writings of Salman Rushdie is an example – as is being tall and blonde, which is often taken to be a natural asset yet is quite the reverse if you are taken to be German in some parts of rural Greece. With respect to the latter, consider a 'naturally gifted' snooker player. Immense holdings flow from the exercise of his natural talent yet in a different time and/or place, he might be viewed with some curiosity – as a man with an impractical stick who is dressed rather like a penguin. Why then does it follow that his is a natural *asset*? It is a natural fact about him that he can play snooker but this only becomes a natural asset or advantage with consequent entitlement to holdings in a snooker-loving jackpot paying society. The natural[14] fact that one can play snooker well, then, only leads to gross entitlements and consequent inequalities in a particular political and economic system.

Given the observations so far, we can clearly see that there is a social component to what we determine and reward as an asset. However, it is not clear that the same can be said of talents. Indeed, dictionary definitions tend to distinguish between 'talent' as mental endowment or natural ability and 'asset', where the emphasis is on the *use* or *value* of a particular thing or person.[15] Given that, we might want to maintain that a talent is a talent whether or not it is or becomes an asset (as in the artist example), which implies that, while assets are to some degree socially defined, talents or abilities need not be. An alternative would be to argue that talents *are* assets and so also, by implication, to some degree socially defined. Whichever way we might like to proceed, the point remains that 'assets', which play a central role in Nozick's theory of entitlement, have a certain if not considerable social component. As such, it is hard to see much that is natural about them, other than their variable relation to natural abilities. Moreover, given that assets are at least partly determined by what sorts of skills we value and what we do indeed value is open to moral critique, then so is the corresponding distribution of supposed entitlements.

Having shown that we can mount a conceptual challenge to the very idea of 'assets' being 'natural', it must be said that there *just do* seem to be things that are naturally advantageous and disadvantageous. Functional limitation, for example, could be held to be naturally disadvantageous and a certain degree of intelligence could be held to be naturally advantageous. However, what could be uncontroversially held to be natural assets or disadvantages comprises a small subset of what are commonly held to be natural assets or disadvantages. We have only to envisage an assumed advantage or dis-advantage in a light where it would become the opposite to dismiss it as being by nature one or the other. The immensely strong man handling delicate antique glassware, the beautiful yet eternally misunderstood woman, the wealthy but lonely entrepreneur and the gifted philosopher in the lunatic asylum are examples where a supposedly natural asset can amount to a disadvantage in one way or another.

However, even if we were to concede that some things may be naturally advantageous and disadvantageous, this does not give much ground to Nozick. This is because, as already suggested, the link between natural advantages and disadvantages and social advantages and disadvantages is neither direct nor inevitable. That is to say, social dis/advantage rarely cor-responds accurately with natural dis/advantage: one need not be naturally dis/advantaged to be socially dis/advantaged, and society can compound natural dis/advantage. Moreover, the link between natural and social dis/advantage is not fixed. A natural dis/advantage *need not* lead to a social dis/advantage: we can question the morality of a system where such relations occur. For example, physical impairment is seen as a natural disadvantage in contemporary society that in turn leads to natural inequalities between those who are disabled and those who are not. However, we have seen that this is too simple. There is clearly a natural inequality between those who are functionally limited and those who are not, yet seeing it as nothing but natural hides both the fact that much disability is compounded if not cre-ated by society, and the fact that much disability can be remedied by social action. The fault lies then in equating disability with a natural and unal-terable state of affairs when much disability amounts to an alterable social disadvantage. So, even if we admit that to a limited extent there are such things as natural advantages and disadvantages, we should be acutely aware of the questionable and alterable nature of the relations between them and social dis/advantages. It is a certain type of society that decides upon and upholds those relations as they presently exist.[16]

If, then, what we assume to be natural can be seriously questioned and the correspondence between natural and social dis/advantages is not direct or unalterable, Nozick's notion of entitlement requires a lot of revision before it can get off the ground. That is to say, if assets are to some degree socially defined and to varying degrees socially rewarded, we should look at the processes by which they are so defined and rewarded before we bestow any legitimacy upon present entitlements. If certain natural capacities or incapacities count as advantages or disadvantages and are rewarded as such for no good reasons, then, by implication, there are no good reasons to allow some, as a result, to benefit from entitlements and others to be excluded from them. Nozick provides no good reason to believe that a free market structure should define what count as assets and handicaps. Although he favours leaving things up to the market, doing so clearly leads to serious deprivations that, as we have seen, are not easy to defend. Indeed, if a free market structure can be seen to unfairly reward or penalise 'natural' assets or impediments, for example, by allowing physical impairment to entail social and economic disadvantages when this is not at all inevitable, then it follows that the whole network of entitlements that flow from such a structure may well be unfair. Moral blindness in the market place may imply that we are not entitled to everything that flows from our supposedly natural assets.

Nozick could counter these difficulties by asserting that the type of social system he advocates (a free market economy with minimal state) is a natural state of affairs, or the most natural state of affairs. It would follow from this that individual features that are advantageous in a natural system could be legitimately called natural assets. That being so, Nozick could run his argument by us again. However, it is questionable as to whether Nozick could come up with any coherent arguments to suggest that a free market economy with a minimal state is *the* natural apparatus for regulating the lives of human beings. He does not argue that a free market economy and minimal state embodies the fulfilment of our human nature. Rather, he realises the inherent difficulty of such an enterprise: 'The completely accurate statement of the moral background, including the precise statement of the moral theory and its underlying basis, would require a full-scale presentation and is a task for another time. (A lifetime?)'.[17] So, without a 'completely accurate statement of the moral background' from which entitlements to the fruits of the exercise of 'natural' assets are derived, the gap in Nozick's theory is sufficiently extensive that we need not accept that most assets are natural, fairly determined or bestow any legitimate consequential entitlement upon their holders.

If we give weight to the suggestion that individual advantages or assets are in many cases not inevitable or natural and that the process of determining what we value and how we reward it should be subject to much further investigation, both Nozick's and Rawls' theories display significant shortcomings. That is, they can be said to fail to question deeply enough the network of assumptions underlying the system that they are proposing to best organise. Rawls, for example, considers the plight of the worst off to be an unalterable natural fact that can only be compensated for via the difference principle. He does not adequately consider the justice of the system that defines what a 'favourable starting place' is, but instead works within a framework and accounts for the inequalities thrown up therein, without challenging it too much. Nozick makes similar short cuts, perhaps in the hope that we will accept his conclusions. We need not accept his conclusions, however, without questioning both what should count as assets or dis/advantages, and what entitlements should flow from them. If this were done, Nozick's theory of entitlement might gain some plausibility, as opposed to justifying the confinement of some people to the margins of society and legitimising the accruing of massive financial holdings by others, like snooker players and Australian soap opera stars who struggle to sing in tune.

The reasons why we should feel obligated to provide in cases of social deprivation have not been extinguished, then, by Nozick's entitlement theory. Those reasons recommend that we not be entitled to *whatever* flows from the exercise of our natural talents. Weaknesses have been identified in the clauses of Nozick's argument. Moreover, his theory is based upon a market-driven and rather unsophisticated conception of natural dis/advantages (as we have seen, for example, not much about them is determined by nature). By implication, there is room for much further enquiry. The process of determining what assets are and how they are rewarded both can and should be questioned. Without further investigation and argument, there is no need to accept that it is at all justified or desirable that the market solely determine such things. More generally, the arguments from preceding chapters add weight to the suggestion that we should resist such a strong emphasis on such a negative conception of freedom where it is at the expense of a rather modest notion of equality or, some might say, humanity. Therefore, all things considered, Nozick's theory does not amount to a watertight method of evading responsibility for the provision of important basic freedoms. In turn, to continue to fail to provide for those freedoms where people are without them remains both unjustified and morally unsettling.

# 9   An argument from democracy

Up to now, many lines of enquiry have been investigated that are directly relevant to the claim that we should be obligated to provide for conditional basic freedoms in cases of social deprivation. It has been contended that none of the challenges to that claim have been successful. A less direct but complementary approach is to look at a commonly accepted ideal, explore the values lying behind it and see what those values imply with regard to other issues, notably disability and deprivation more generally. This is the approach taken up here. The aim is to conclude this part of the book by consolidating the arguments that have been presented so far.

Henceforth, the commonly accepted ideal of democracy will be explored. It will be suggested that all models of democracy ultimately rely on the same justification. That justification lies in the ideal of self-government tethered to the ideal of equality of respect for persons. It will be argued that respect for such ideals both coheres with and adds support to the claim that we should be obligated to provide for conditional basic freedoms in the cases of relative social deprivation and socially induced disability. If we believe in the value of democracy, it is inconsistent to remain unsympathetic to the arguments of previous chapters.

Exploring the justification of democracy necessitates that we first define it. Democracy is a term that can both portray a value and be used descriptively. It literally means people rule.[1] The idea of rule by the people must therefore be adhered to if a particular description or inter- pretation is to warrant calling itself a description or interpretation of democ- racy. It is this basic idea that requires justification, however it is interpreted and whatever it is taken to imply. 'It says nothing about elections, or representation. It does not indicate who comprise "the people" ... it is an idea that can be easily qualified or diluted ... Nevertheless, it is necessarily the central element in any plausible conception of democracy.'[2] Qualifica- tions and dilutions aside, we must ask why this central element is taken to be a good thing, that is, how rule by the people is justified as an appropriate way by which to live. I will briefly look at justifications of democracy that seem to avoid recourse to any ideal at all and show that ultimately they do not. Doing that will expose the ideals upon which the justification of democracy is based. The ramifications of those ideals can then be explored.

The first justifications of democracy to consider are of a practical nature. The reasons that comprise these justifications do not necessarily imply one another, but they all tend to stress the consequences of democratic procedure rather than the desirability of the procedure in itself. Hence, they are all broadly negative. Indeed, some border on the cynical. One such reason in support of democracy is that there is not a feasible non-democratic alternative. 'A hard-headed look at human experience, shows that among political societies that have actually existed, or now exist, those that most nearly satisfy the criteria of the democratic idea are, taken all round, better than the rest.'[3] The emphasis here is on democracy as the lesser evil when compared to the alternatives. The burden of proof[4] lies with the alternatives to show that there are coherent and favourable grounds for rejecting democracy.

Some theorists are more optimistic and take the above argument further. Rather than relying on 'the rest' being undesirable, democracy is taken to have its own desirable consequences, even if the most basic of these is that it provides safeguards against what is undesirable. That is to say, whether democracies tend to produce just government or not, they at least tend to prevent serious injustice.[5] Serious injustice is often taken to mean tyrannical rule, with democracy being justified in so far as it provides safeguards against the emergence of tyrannical rulers. If power rests with the people, the argument goes, the cruel and arbitrary use of authority will be averted, even if all this amounts to is 'voters having the right, at periodic intervals, to remove from office governments that they have come to dislike'.[6] Indeed, Riker argues that all that we can expect from democracy is a popular veto by which it is 'sometimes possible to restrain official tyranny'.[7] That aside, it is held that the justification of democracy, as being the best defence against tyranny, 'could serve as the sufficient and only defence for anyone who is not prepared to defend tyranny'.[8]

As well as safeguarding against tyranny, democracy is held to have further desirable consequences. Nelson argues, for example, that democracy is desirable due to the fact that it tends to produce good laws and policies, or at least to prevent bad ones.[9] Dahl is more specific, asserting that democracy tends to provide a more extensive domain of personal freedom than any other kind of regime can promise. He argues that certain valuable rights including rights to free expression, political organisation, opposition and fair and free elections are essential to the democratic process. Moreover:

> these fundamental political rights are unlikely to exist in isolation. The political culture required to support the democratic order ... tends to emphasise the value of personal rights, freedoms and opportunities. Thus not only as an ideal but in actual practice, the democratic process is surrounded by a penumbra of personal freedom.[10]

Dahl's optimism here is still very tentative. At best, democracy is said to tend to promote a broad range of human freedom. If this is not realised, democracy is still defensible through recourse to the desirability of safe-guarding against tyranny and, at the very least, we can comfort ourselves with the knowledge that there are not any desirable or feasible alternatives. These broadly negative reasons given in support of democracy identify nothing of value in the idea of democracy itself. We can thereby ask whe-ther they amount to enough to justify democracy.

If there is nothing else to recommend democracy other than the absence of desirable or feasible alternatives, we might not feel that we have justified democracy at all. Indeed, such a justification would be based on the highly contingent prediction that a more desirable and feasible alternative will not be forthcoming. This does not seem to be congruent with democracy being highly valued. There is nothing to recommend democracy as an ideal or a process in itself. There is no reference to the justice implicit in the demo-cratic ideal. Consequently, it can be said that this notion does not justify democracy: it merely amounts to a highly relative vindication.[11]

What about the idea that democracy provides a safeguard against tyr-anny? The justifying force of this is determined by the extent to which tyr-anny is seen to be a bad thing and, thus, the extent to which its avoidance is seen to be of value. If the cruel and arbitrary use of authority is seen to be a fundamental evil and democracy 'tends' to safeguard against that use, then we might be in a position to say that democracy is justified by the ideal of non-tyrannical rule. However, even if we were to concede this, it would not get us very far. The question would remain unanswered as to why tyranny is seen to be a bad thing. Further investigation along this trail will uncover the values that are implicit in the assumption that tyranny is bad and, by implication, the deeper ideals that serve to justify democracy.

There must be something about tyranny to which we are deeply averse. Rather than simple distaste, it is plausible to assume that our wish to avoid tyrannical rule is motivated by the belief that we should not be bypassed or oppressed, that despotism violates us in some way. There must then be some-thing that we value which tyranny jeopardises and democracy respects. It fol-lows from this that the motivation to have that something of value respected ultimately provides the reason to endorse democracy and to reject tyranny. The outcome of democratic procedure respects what tyrannical rule does not. Now unless the idea of democracy has an arbitrary relation to the outcome of democratic procedure, it must also respect whatever it is that we hold to be of value. This in turn implies that, if our adherence to democracy is based on the fact that the idea of democracy and the result of democratic proce-dures (that is, non-tyranny) respect whatever it is that we hold to be of value, democracy may indeed be justified by its respect for that very same thing.

Rather than looking to what democracy is supposed to be safeguarding against, then, we should look at the values that those safeguards imply. The outcome of democratic methods must ultimately reflect an ideal and, unless the outcome is incidental, it should reflect the democratic ideal. That democracy safeguards against tyranny only tells half of the story, to the neglect of the values implicit in the motivation to make such a safeguard. In order to complete the story we must therefore discover what values are implied by the rejection of tyranny, that is, what values justify that we be democratic instead.

The rejection of tyranny implies the belief that the unjustified coercion of individuals is wrong. The idea of rule by the people could thus be said, as opposed to tyranny, to respect individuals as ends in themselves rather than mere means to the ends of a tyrannous few, hence Dahl's tentative optimism with regard to the propensity of democracy to extend the realm of personal freedom. Indeed, the political rights identified by Dahl as being essential to the democratic process can be seen to ensure that people are not treated as mere means.[12] That people should be treated as ends in themselves and thus be free is a suitable candidate, then, for the idea that drives and justifies democracy. It is the idea that people should be self-governing, that every person must be respected as a source of claims and not be treated as a mere instrument. 'Democracy ... is a recognition that no authority can be keeper of a man's conscience.'[13]

Cohen argues that the essence of democracy is self-government or, when expressed as a moral ideal, autonomy.[14] We can take the terms autonomy (self-law) and self-government to be interchangeable, as there is no difference that is relevant here between the freedom and capacity to govern one's own life and pursue one's own ends in one's own ways (self-government) and the capacity to 'reason self-consciously, to be self reflective and to be self determining' (autonomy).[15] Cohen asserts that, as in no other system of government, the principle of autonomy is clearly and fully embodied in democracy:

> Community autonomy – the inter-personal correlate of autonomy in the life of the individual – is fully realised only when the community is democratically governed. Only under democracy do the members of the community at large develop their own rules governing joint affairs, and impose these rules upon themselves ... the autonomous character of democratic government is its most fundamental and perhaps most important feature.[16]

Held similarly argues that the different aspirations of liberal and New Left democratic theorists are all linked by the concept of autonomy, that in all cases the justification of democracy lies in the ideal of self-government. 'The specification of the conditions of enactment of the principle of autonomy amounts to the specification of the conditions for the participation of citizens in decisions about issues which are important to them.'[17] He argues that the principle of autonomy therefore requires that political society be democratically organised.

Given the above, democracy can be seen to follow directly from the ideal of self-government or autonomy. Rule by the people is the natural expression of self-government in society. However, it would be premature to open the bar. If self-government or autonomy were an absolute ideal, it is unclear as to whether any form of government could follow from it, let alone democracy. That is to say, 'with government, even democracies, laws come to someone from the outside. The individual citizens have to do things because they are the law, even if it is a law which they helped in creating ... once people engage in a community and are bound by that community's decisions, then to that extent they lose their autonomy'.[18] Given this, we would only seem to be left with recourse to a somewhat negative defence of democracy, that it violates the ideal of self-government less than any feasible alternative. If this were true, we might still be able to argue that the justification of democracy does lie in the ideal of self-government. However, it is not at all obvious that it is.

The ideal of self-government is dealt a democratic blow given the tendency of democracies to endorse the principle that 'where there cannot be universal agreement, matters should be settled according to the will or wishes of the majority'.[19] This effectively means that the ideal of self-government will not be respected by democracy where there is a minority. The autonomy of a minority will be compromised for the sake of the autonomy of the majority.

Furthermore, as Harrison notes, there is a sense in which the self-government of individual members of a majority is sacrificed through democracy:

> In a democracy it is true that the individual members of the majority do choose the result which in fact happens. But it does not happen just because they individually choose it. It only happens because a certain number of other people want it as well. Of course each person does have input into the decision procedure. But so in this sense, do the individual members of the minority.[20]

Whether justified by the ideal of self-government or not, then, if all democracy amounts to is that everyone has an input into a decision procedure that has the effect it does because of the input of others, only a minimal notion of self-government can be satisfied by democracy.

However, one might still maintain that democracy safeguards more autonomy than any other feasible alternative, especially if we admit that autonomy should not be taken to be an absolute ideal.[21] That is to say, given that the realisation of self-government as an absolute ideal can be seen to be incompatible with any form of government, democracy is still a good candidate for being the system that secures more autonomy than any other. Even though the realisation of one's self-governing choices is dependent on the choices of others, at least democracy has the effect that the self-governing choices of those comprising the majority are reflected in a decision. Moreover, it is said to safeguard the individual rights and freedoms cited earlier as essential to the democratic process. Such rights and freedoms are in turn essential to real choice. Democracy could thus be said to respect individual autonomy more than other systems since it secures the conditions of individual choice and, 'more often than not', it will allow an individual's choices to be effective. If autonomy is a good, 'democracy is a good thing, and its promotion of autonomy is why it is a good thing'.[22]

However, we are still faced with the problem of the compromising of the autonomy of a given minority. They would be unlikely to agree that democracy safeguards their autonomy or that it at least reflects their autonomous choices more than any other feasible alternative. This is especially true in the case of permanent minorities whereby the majority will always tend to have the advantage. In this case, members of the permanent minority may find that their choices are never effective, that democracy gives them no opportunity whatsoever to govern themselves. 'From the point of view of this permanent minority ... democracy gives them no more control than an oligarchy would.'[23] This extreme case is indicative of the more general difficulty that whenever I am in the minority, what I think ought to happen will not happen. To the extent that my living autonomously requires that I do what I believe I ought to do, democracy will bypass or violate my autonomy whenever I am in the minority. It will require that I abide by a majority decision that I believe to be wrong. If self-government is an ideal essential to the justification of democracy, then, we may justly ask why democracy requires that I defer to a majority of which I am not a part. The answer to this question will show that the justification of democracy does not lie solely in the ideal of self-government.

We have seen that democracy purports to respect the idea that people should be treated as ends in themselves rather than as means to the ends of a tyrannous few. Yet a conflict has been unearthed between the ideal of self-government and democracy. The ideal of self-government can potentially gain very little expression through democracy. However, this does not entail that democracy disrespects the idea that people should be treated as ends in themselves. Rather, the opposite is the case. Democracy requires that *all* people should be treated as ends in themselves. This in turn necessitates that we show an equality of respect to all other people.

> If all moral agents are to be equally respected, then I must give weight (or moral consideration) to everyone expressing their moral views. If they are doing so by voting, then I should give these votes equal respect. If I give these votes equal respect, then the view I should respect as superior is the view supported by the majority. Every vote counts equally and that is the view with more votes.[24]

It is this consideration that requires that we compromise our autonomy. Democracy embodies the idea that 'when binding decisions are made, the claims of each citizen as to the laws, rules, policies, etc. to be adopted must be counted as valid and equally valid'.[25] That all interests must be weighed impartially gives the reason to respect a majority view, 'quite independently of any view I myself have about the truth of the matter'.[26]

Harrison argues that the conception of equality fundamental to the idea of democracy is a 'kind of second order equality': 'It doesn't say that goods should be distributed equally. It doesn't even directly recommend egalitarian practical procedures. But it does say that, when considering anything at all, equal respect should be given to all moral agents.'[27] This idea of natural equality pays homage to the Christian belief that the redeemer died for all, that we are all God's children. Democracy is justified to a large extent by this: 'once the idea of the natural equality of men has got about, claims to rule cannot be based on natural superiority'.[28] Without equality, there is no reason to believe that democracy is an appropriate ideal or method by which to rule. 'Only with liberty will democracy work, but only with equality is there reason to believe it ought to work.'[29] So, although we have seen that the justification of democracy does lie in the ideal of self-government, the ideal of self-government is regulated by the ideal of equality of respect for persons. Given this, the justification of democracy must lie in both the ideal of self-government and the ideal of equality of respect for persons.[30]

Although the ideal of self-government is regulated by the ideal of equality of respect for persons, equality of respect will also protect self-government. As Harrison argues, the equality of respect for persons gives us a reason to follow the majority view (sometimes at the expense of our autonomy), but it will also imply fundamental rights that should be secured to each person whatever the majority might say. Since equality of respect provides a reason as to why we should be democratic,

> democracy should not be allowed to do anything that conflicts with such respect. We may therefore shield individuals with rights to prevent such depredations by the majority. This may be undemocratic; but it is as morally justified as democracy itself is.[31]

This argument has implications both generally and specifically with regard to social deprivation.

The arguments so far add up to the fact that, if we believe that democracy is justified rather than vindicated, we must also believe in the ideal of equality of respect for persons. That ideal will both regulate and protect our autonomy. It follows from this that, at the very least, the conditions of self-government ought to be safeguarded for all, including those who find themselves in a minority. Equality of respect might further necessitate that society be more sensitive with regard to the plight of permanent minorities. That the provision of conditional basic freedoms would go some way to ensuring that the conditions of self-government would be safeguarded for all is not a controversial claim to make. Even though we are talking about a 'kind of second order equality' here, it can be seen to have more direct practical implications, the more seriously we take it. For example, it is a necessary condition for the realisation of both equality of respect for persons and self-government, as we know it, that people have a roof over their heads. The same can be said about basic freedoms to do with education, health care and mobility. To deny that, borrowing from Pogge, is to deny the fundamental role that basic social and economic needs actually play in a human life.[32] Indeed, given the level of affluence and prosperity of British society, the provision of conditional basic freedoms for all could be said to amount to a rather modest expression of equality of respect.

Thus, we have only to expose the sympathies intrinsic to the commonly held ideal of democracy to see that provision ought to be made in the cases of relative social deprivation and, more specifically, socially induced disability. Provision should be made as an expression of equality of respect that secures the conditions of self-government. At the very least, an extension of those sympathies serves to highlight the reprehensibility of our failure to provide. Moreover, we should be sympathetic to the circumstances of people who are socially deprived in so far as they constitute permanent minorities. A lack of sympathy for the 14 per cent of the adult population who experience disability, the 8 per cent of the population who live below the poverty line and the conservatively estimated 10,000 rough sleepers, for example, tends to ensure that they remain marginalised. Their choices are rarely effective if indeed they are registered (a further aspect of our failure to include). Provision in these cases would encourage that the penumbra of personal freedom that Dahl lauds as surrounding the democratic process becomes an actuality for more than a very fortunate majority.

It has been argued that justifications of the commonly accepted ideal of democracy ultimately appeal to a value. Efficacy is no justification. The ideal of self-government tethered to the ideal of equality of respect for persons determines what we judge to be efficacious and in turn justifies that we be democratic. Without reference to these ideals, the concept of democracy is rather vacuous. Advocates of all models of democracy must presume that 'the people' can and should govern: that they can requires autonomy and that they should respects equality. Moreover, we have seen that endorsing such ideals reinforces the claim that we should be obligated to establish conditional basic freedoms in cases of relative social deprivation and socially induced disability. To continue to fail to provide in these cases is not nearly consistent with a true valuing of or respect for others.

# Part Three

# Augmenting reason

## Introduction

I hope to have established so far that there are very good reasons to stop allowing the considerable hardship of people around us. This part of the book considers the possibility that compelling arguments recommending that we should not continue to allow serious relative social deprivation and socially induced disablement might have little *effect* whatsoever. Given that we are talking about a considerable and a remediable inequality of human freedom, it is of some concern that the philosophical argument hitherto presented might not be very successful at motivating social change. It is worth considering, then, whether those arguments can be helped along a bit via other sources of insight and understanding.

## Is reason underpowered? The story of Mrs Smith

Many years ago I met a woman called Mrs Smith. She had just been discharged from hospital after surviving a rather harrowing illness. Indeed, for a time it had been uncertain whether she would live. She was radiant and obviously enjoying her return to normal life with restored health. During the course of the conversation, she described her delight at renewing relations with her daughter. Previous to her illness she had not seen or spoken to her daughter for five years. This was due to her reaction to her daughter's clandestine association with a married man. Mrs Smith described how being unwell had made her realise what was important in life; it put things in perspective. She reasoned that she had been rather petty, rigid and short-sighted and that nothing should have kept her from the joys of the mother–daughter relationship. No longer was she going to forfeit the depth of reciprocal affection and love bound up with that relationship. Mrs Smith had already missed the birth of her first grandchild, something that she regretted bitterly, and she was not about to miss out again. After all, she considered her family to be the most important thing in her life and her role as a mother definitive of who she was as a human being.

While I was glad that Mrs Smith had re-established contact with her daughter, I could not help but feel a little unsettled by her story. She had divulged what she considered to be very good reasons to renew contact with her daughter. Why had it taken a tragedy to unearth them? And, if Mrs Smith had already unearthed them, why had she not been prompted to act differently prior to falling ill? Whatever the case, Mrs Smith had not been previously motivated to change her ways. It took a rather excessive jolt to do that. It intrigued me why a tragedy should have so much more power than human thought. I wondered whether a prior warning of her impending illness would by itself have been enough to motivate her to change. If that were the case, then it would be conceivable that the very thought of, for example, a tragedy, rather than its actual occurrence, would be sufficient to have an effect on human action. I speculated that, if she had unearthed them, Mrs Smith's reasons did not have the motivational force of a tragedy, nor perhaps even of the thought of one. If she had not thought of any reasons to reconcile with her daughter, then Mrs Smith's illness changed both her mind and her motivation. Either way, reason alone was rather weak in this case.

Given the compelling nature of the arguments in favour of making more social provision presented in the preceding chapters, the object of the following chapters is to supply those arguments with some motivational force or zest. If the above example is anything to go by, then giving many reasons why we should make more social provision in cases of social deprivation will not necessarily motivate us *to* provide. So, rather than waiting for tragedy (or more tragedy) to strike, it might be fruitful if a theoretical approach were wedded to, if you like, good PR. The idea of subsequent chapters, then, is both to attempt to motivate action (supply the PR) with respect to social deprivation and to explore the notion that philosophical theory can incorporate and be augmented by other sources of understanding.

Chapters 10 and 11 explore the rich resources provided by the work of Nietzsche. I do not purport to be at all faithful to Nietzsche's project; nor am I contending that this is *the* contribution that Nietzsche's work makes. I am merely suggesting that his writing can be used legitimately in this context and that such use is profitable in so far as it is provocative and illuminating with respect to our understanding of others. Indeed, it will be shown that Nietzsche's writing can arrest us to the plight of others by making their circumstances intrinsic to the evaluation of our own lives. Furthermore, his genealogy of morality enriches our understanding of human hardship. In so far as it does this, it should help to motivate us to *do* something about the hardships that are the concern of this book. Chapter 12 looks at additional sources of understanding that might similarly motivate us. It explores the idea that the novelist, the poet and the journalist might be better at sensitising us to the experiences of others than the theoretician. Using such sources within a theoretical framework might thereby help to motivate us to act upon the compelling reasons that we have to provide in cases of social deprivation.

# 10 Nietzsche's thought experiment
## The idea of eternal recurrence

Nietzsche thought the idea of eternal recurrence to be his most fundamental conception. If Mrs Smith had come across it, there is an added chance that she might have changed her ways sooner than she did. The idea of eternal recurrence can be seen as a test about the attitude that we have towards our temporally finite lives and the attitude that we have towards the world more generally. It offers an alternative way of approaching some of the issues hitherto discussed and has the propensity to enliven them. It does this by making the conditions of the world in which we live intrinsic to the evaluation of our own lives. So, if we affirm our own lives, we must also affirm a society where remediable deprivations and disabilities, for example, are commonplace. In getting us to think in this way, Nietzsche's test makes the plight of others more immediate. As well as being motivated to do something about our own lives, we might thereby be motivated to do something about the conditions in which others live.

Before turning to the question of what the idea of eternal recurrence has to offer us, it has to be established that the idea really is intended as a thought experiment. This cannot be assumed. Indeed, it is often levelled against Nietzsche's doctrine of eternal recurrence that it merely constitutes a crude cosmological or metaphysical hypothesis. It will be shown, however, that there is a certain lack of cosmological proof in Nietzsche's published work and that any such proof is very troublesome. It will further be shown that the literal truth of the doctrine of eternal recurrence is unimportant and that, moreover, the truth of the doctrine would impede its assumption of the central role assigned to it by Nietzsche in his philosophy. The power of the idea of eternal recurrence lies in its being read creatively.

Cosmological proof pertaining to the literal truth of the idea of eternal recurrence is lacking in Nietzsche's published work. Indeed, it is difficult to find evidence that he considered it to be a cosmology at all. The idea of eternal recurrence is articulated in such a way so as to sound cosmological in *Thus Spoke Zarathustra*.[1] In the section entitled 'The Convalescent', Zarathustra confronts his 'most abysmal thought' and has to lie down for seven days. After this period, his animals hail him as the teacher of eternal recurrence, speaking thus:

Everything goes, everything returns; the wheel of existence rolls for ever. Everything dies, everything blossoms anew; the year of existence runs on for ever. Everything breaks, everything is joined anew; the same house of existence builds itself for ever. Everything departs, everything meets again; the ring of existence is true to itself for ever ... Behold we know what you teach: that all things recur eternally and we ourselves with them, and that we have already existed an infinite number of times before and all things with us. You teach that there is a great year of becoming, a colossus of a year: this year must, like an hour-glass, turn itself over again and again, so that it may run down and run out anew.[2]

This could be taken to be the presentation of a somewhat bizarre cosmology. However, Zarathustra's response to his animals suggests otherwise:

O you buffoons and barrel organs! ... how well you know what had to be fulfilled in seven days: and how that monster crept into my throat and choked me! But I bit its head off and spat it away. And you – have already made a hurdy-gurdy song out of it? I, however, lie here now, still weary from this biting away, still sick with my own redemption.[3]

The animals may have constructed a crude cosmology from Zarathustra's abysmal thought, but have failed to grasp the psychological subtleties that make such a thought abysmal. As will be seen later, if Zarathustra's abysmal thought was indeed an eternal recurrence as cosmology, he would be hard pressed to explain why such a thought was so repulsive in the absence of psychological continuity. We should also remember that this articulation of what would seem to be a cosmological idea is being uttered by a group of animals in a work of fiction. Zarathustra has nothing to do with the idea in this form.

What could Zarathustra's abysmal thought be, then, if not the cosmology of eternal recurrence? It could be the thought that to affirm one's recurrence entails that one affirm the recurrence of all the bad and repulsive parts of life too, which, for Zarathustra, is the eternal recurrence of the 'little man'.

A long twilight limps in front of me, a mortally-weary, death intoxicated sadness which speaks with a yawn. "The man of whom you are weary, the little man, recurs eternally" – thus my sadness yawned and dragged its feet and could not fall asleep.[4]

Nehamas similarly identifies Zarathustra's abysmal thought with the idea that, if he affirms his own eternal recurrence, he must affirm the eternal recurrence of the 'small man'.

Zarathustra is disgusted with the thought that this contemptible type, who asks "What is love? What is creation? What is longing? What is a star? ... and ... blinks" (Z, Pref., 5), is ineliminable and will never cease to exist. We do not need to suppose that the world repeats itself infinitely in order to explain Zarathustra's disgust.[5]

It follows then that if Zarathustra affirms the repetition of his own life, he has, by implication, to affirm the repetition of that with which his life has been concerned. The idea of the eternal recurrence of the 'small man' is so abysmal because he has spent a great part of a book teaching that man is 'something that should be overcome'. Cosmological reality is superfluous here; what is important is the psychological impact of such an idea when one realises what it involves. Clark argues that, in realising that the affirmation of life entails affirmation of eternal recurrence, including the recurrence of the small man, Zarathustra 'realises his own distance from the ideal that he has been preaching'.[6] That aside, both Clark and Nehamas agree that the idea of the recurrence of 'the smallest' need not require belief in its real possibility.

There is another problematic passage in *Zarathustra* which suggests that the idea of eternal recurrence does not amount to a creative psychological experiment. It is where Zarathustra confronts his 'spirit of gravity' with an account of recurrence. The account sounds suspiciously cosmological. Indeed, Nehamas cites this as the 'clearest statement of the cosmological version of recurrence among Nietzsche's published texts'.[7]

> From this gateway moment a long, eternal lane runs back: an eternity lies behind us. Must not all things that can run have already run along this lane? Must not all things that can happen have already happened, been done, run past? And if all things have been here before: what do you think of this moment, dwarf? Must not this gateway, too, have been here – before? ... And this slow spider that creeps along in the moonlight, and this moonlight itself, and I and you at this gateway whispering together, whispering of eternal things – must we not all have been here before? ... And ... must we not return eternally?[8]

Zarathustra certainly frightens off his spirit of gravity with this statement and Nehamas asserts that he tells such a story with the sole purpose of doing so. Indeed, the emphasis of the whole passage is psychological: if its purpose were a cold description of a cosmological theory of eternal recurrence, then Zarathustra's spirit of gravity need not have been so frightened and have made such a swift exit. Moreover, the imagery of Zarathustra's vision portrayed later in the same passage, of the shepherd who bites the head off the heaviest blackest snake and springs up a transformed being, hints at the psychological effect that Zarathustra sees to be synonymous with the affirmation of eternal recurrence.

In addition, no proof is offered in this passage with regard to the cosmological truth of eternal recurrence. Nehamas argues that Zarathustra does not himself believe that what he is saying to his spirit of gravity holds any truth.

> If he does, why does Nietzsche write in 'The Convalescent', which occurs considerably later in this work, that Zarathustra has not yet taught the recurrence? Could it be that Zarathustra tells the story only in order to frighten off the dwarf, while the psychological implications Nietzsche wants to draw from it presuppose only a weaker hypothesis?[9]

Zarathustra is certainly tentative in the text about just what it is that he is saying to the dwarf: 'Thus I spoke, and I spoke more and more softly: for I was afraid of my own thoughts and reservations.'[10] This suggests that we should not attribute belief in the cosmological truth of the idea of eternal recurrence to Zarathustra and, since the clearest cosmological expression of the idea is found here, we can further assert that 'the published texts reveal no unambiguous commitment to a recurrence cosmology, much less arguments for one'.[11]

However, Nietzsche's unpublished texts do suggest that the idea of eternal recurrence can only amount to a crude cosmological or metaphysical hypothesis. In *The Will to Power*[12] Nietzsche offers us an argument in support of recurrence as a cosmological hypothesis.

> If the world may be thought of as a certain definite quantity of force and as a certain definite number of centers of force ... it follows that in the great dice game of existence, it must pass through a calculable number of combinations. In infinite time, every possible combination would at some time or another be realised; more: it would be realised an infinite number of times. And ... between every combination and its next recurrence all other possible combinations would have to take place.[13]

Nehamas argues that at least two premises are necessary to Nietzsche's position here: that the sum total of energy in the universe is finite and that the total number of energy states in the universe is finite. He contends that Nietzsche is mistaken in assuming that the first premise entails the second: 'A system may have only a finite amount of energy, and yet that total can be distributed in an infinite number of ways; this would then prevent the repetition that Nietzsche may have had in mind.'[14]

Schacht argues further that, even if we assume that the total number of energy states in the universe is finite, 'these suppositions by themselves entail neither that "every possible combination" would occur an "infinite number of times", nor even that "every possible combination" would actually occur'.[15] He makes the additional point that it does not follow from Nietzsche's position that 'between every combination and its next recurrence all other combinations would have to take place'. 'That is either an arbitrary stipulation or a point requiring strong independent argument, the very possibility of which is highly dubious ... moreover ... nothing would directly follow about the order in which the combinations would occur.'[16] We should conclude from this that the arguments that Nietzsche offers in support of a cosmological thesis of eternal recurrence are highly dubious. Furthermore, the a priori nature of such arguments, if we take them seriously, directly conflicts with Nietzsche's scorn for metaphysics.

As well as being highly dubious, the cosmological thesis of eternal recurrence is rather uninteresting. That is to say, the literal truth of a recurrence cosmology would entail that its psychological effect be less intense than Nietzsche supposes. If we were to literally 'return eternally to this identical and self-same life', that it be 'identical and self-same' requires that we have no knowledge of returning. We would not be going through it again: each life, in order to be the self-same life, would have to be the first and only life psychologically. We may be justly unconcerned then with real eternal recurrence, since we cannot remember going through this before and we will not remember going through it again. The thought of literal eternal recurrence would lead us to question, if at all, whether we wanted to give someone else a fulfilling or tedious life. We need not care very much that our lives have happened an infinite number of times before, and that they will happen an infinite number of times in the future makes little difference with regard to the attitude that we should have towards them now. So, if the idea of eternal recurrence amounts to a (highly dubious) cosmological hypothesis, Nietzsche cannot coherently think that the idea constitutes a heavy burden.

However, Nietzsche clearly did not believe that the idea of eternal recurrence was a matter of indifference. Therefore, either he misunderstood the ramifications of his most fundamental conception or he did not intend the idea of eternal recurrence to be taken literally. Assuming that the former is tremendously unlikely, we can assert that the thought of eternal recurrence does not amount to thought of what *real* eternal recurrence would be like. Rather, the idea of eternal recurrence is to be digested creatively, as a certain kind of thought experiment.

The idea of eternal recurrence becomes more fruitful and 'makes a much more serious claim to our attention' when read unrealistically as a psychological test of affirmation. Clark describes the idea of eternal recurrence as taking

> the willingness to re-live one's life as a measure of the affirmation of one's nonrecurring life ... this willingness cannot function as a measure of affirmation unless one imagines recurrence unrealistically, on the model of a later occurrence in one's present life.[17]

Viewing eternal recurrence in this way enables us to make sense of the responses to the idea that Nietzsche envisages in *The Gay Science*.[18] This is an earlier articulation of the idea than that found in *Zarathustra* and has no cosmological tone. It does not require the cosmology and could even be said to necessitate its absence.

> What, if some day or night a demon were to steal after you into your loneliest loneliness and say to you: 'This life as you now live it and have lived it, you will have to live once more and innumerable times more; and there will be nothing new in it, but every pain and every joy and every thought and sigh and everything unutterably small or great in your life will have to return to you, all in the same succession and sequence – even this spider and this moonlight between the trees, and even this moment and I myself. The eternal hourglass of existence is turned upside down again and again, and you with it, speck of dust!'
>
> Would you not throw yourself down and gnash your teeth and curse the demon who spoke thus? Or have you once experienced a tremendous moment when you would have answered him: 'You are a god and never have I heard anything more divine.' If this thought gained possession of you, it would change you as you are or perhaps crush you. The question in each and every thing, "Do you desire this once more and innumerable times more?" would lie upon your actions as the greatest weight. Or how well disposed would you have to become to yourself and to life *to crave nothing more fervently* than this ultimate eternal confirmation and seal?[19]

This extraordinary passage sets out Nietzsche's challenge in poetic yet blatant terms. He is not interested in the cosmological feasibility of the idea, but in 'the attitude one must have toward oneself in order to react with joy and not despair to the possibility the demon raises'.[20] Joy and despair only make sense as responses to Nietzsche's test 'if one plays the game and imagines the recurrence of one's life as continuous with and therefore as adding suffering and joy to one's present life'.[21]

Reading Nietzsche's doctrine of eternal recurrence as a certain kind of thought experiment, then, gives the idea its most powerful expression. We must thereby ask what it is that is being tested by such a thought experiment. Inquiry in this direction will inform us of what kinds of issues are enlivened by such a thought experiment and whether Nietzsche has grounds to believe that it constitutes 'the greatest weight'.

Of fundamental importance to the idea of eternal recurrence is its emphasis on the affirmation of life as it really is in this world. The thought of living life innumerable times more with nothing new in it rules out anything other than living life for its own sake, as an end in itself rather than as a means to something else. 'Finding intrinsic value in life itself, that is, valuing the process of living as an end, becomes the only alternative to despair.'[22] This reinforces Nietzsche's stance against ascetic self-denial and what he sees to be repressive Christian morality. Furthermore, affirmation of eternal recurrence requires that we have no regret or, at least, that we can somehow affirm it. Nietzsche's demon places a large emphasis on self-responsibility; it is those who are aware of wasting their time, do many things that they would not want to relive and, by implication, regret much of their lives, that would be frightened by the demon's message. Such fright is intended to be:

> an incentive for man to raise his state of being ... instead of relying on heavenly powers to redeem him, to give meaning to his life and to justify the world, he gives meaning to his life by achieving perfection and exulting in every moment.[23]

Mrs Smith might very well be alarmed then at the thought of eternal recurrence: she would have to eternally return to five years of life without her daughter in it – and a situation where she willingly forfeited the chance to see the birth of her first grandchild. More generally, we might very well gnash our teeth at the thought of eternal recurrence due to the unrealised hopes, wasted opportunities and profound sadnesses with which our lives can be peppered. Nietzsche's test kindly reminds us that we have only ourselves to blame for not thinking in the terms of the test of eternal recurrence before leading a life that we find impossible to affirm.[24] Yet what about sheer bad luck? It seems unlikely that Mrs Smith could affirm the repetition of her serious illness.[25] Likewise, the talented guitarist's thought of eternally returning to the moment where he somewhat foolishly let his concentration slip while chopping kindling wood, putting an end to any hopes of a musical career, may justly make him gnash his teeth, one would think. The requirement of Nietzsche's test here, to affirm the innumerable repetition of every pain, could be said at the very least to demean the tragic and intolerable nature of some pain.[26] Furthermore, it overlooks the possibility of affirming a tragic life while wishing not to repeat it. Nietzsche misses this subtle difference with his rather ferocious formulation.

Clark has similar reservations. She interprets Nietzsche's ideal of affirming eternal recurrence as being a requirement to love the whole process enough that one is willing to relive eternally even those parts of it that one does not and cannot love. However, she asks:

> Why cannot I affirm life precisely by preferring a history stripped of its horrors ... Why isn't it a greater affirmation of life to want the repetition of the past without the bad things? That I cannot recur unless all the horrors do too does not seem like a very good or a very Nietzschean answer.[27]

Clark argues that the affirmation of eternal recurrence is perfectly compatible with preferring that certain things in the world be absent, given the choice. So, our guitarist can reasonably prefer not to have taken his eye off the axe according to Clark.

However, this might be said to be cheating by Nietzsche and arguably misses the point of his thought experiment. The whole point of his doctrine and the reason why he thinks that it constitutes such a heavy burden is that it requires that we affirm bad luck, tragedy and the like. It requires that we face up to and affirm all the horrors of the world. Not only is Mrs Smith encouraged to think about her personal regrets, then, she is encouraged to think about what she might find impossible to affirm in the society and the world in which she lives. In *The Will to Power*, Nietzsche argues that 'everything is so bound up with everything else, that to want to exclude something means to exclude everything. A reprehensible action means: a reprehended world'.[28] Thus, as Nehamas argues, Nietzsche's test requires that

> if I accept any part of myself and my life, then I accept everything about it, and everything about the whole world as well; but if I reject any part, however small and insignificant, then I reject my entire life and all the world with it.[29]

Nehamas argues further that this idea is augmented by Nietzsche's belief that through a new way of life, even the past can be changed; that the state of one's present self affects the very nature of one's past. He cites Zarathustra's words: 'The will is a creator. All "it was" is a fragment, a riddle, a dreadful accident – until the creative will says to it, "But thus I will it; thus shall I will it."'[30] This idea of redeeming through creativity 'all that has been' is very romantic, yet the formerly talented guitarist might find such an idea at best insensitive. Such is the burden of the idea of eternal recurrence. It is testing whether we can affirm both every pain of our own life and every horror of the whole world.

We might not thank Nietzsche here for bowling a psychological googly that seems only to have the effect of deflating us. However, Nietzsche is not out to simply make us feel bad. Indeed, our propensity to feel punctured might tell us something. If we find the prospect of affirming *both* our own life and the whole world alarming, then, assuming that we have a reasonable amount of time left, the test of eternal recurrence points to the fact that we have the ability to make both our own life and the whole world something that can be affirmed. If Nietzsche did not have transformation in mind, it is not at all obvious why the idea of eternal recurrence would lie upon our actions as the greatest weight – why such a thought might change us. So, if we feel that we would not accept the idea of eternal recurrence due to, for example, the feeling that we have wasted a lot of our time and our comprehension of the world as a rather nasty place, then Nietzsche's test implores us to work to change the way that we feel about ourselves and the world. Now although our reaction to the idea of eternal recurrence could change to a certain extent through a shift in attitude towards our life and the world, it is more likely that our reaction would change if we actually did something about our life and the world. We might, for example, attempt both to cease wasting our time and to make the world a less nasty place. On Nietzsche's account, we would then stand a better chance of becoming suitably disposed to ourselves and to life so as to crave nothing more fervently than his ultimate eternal confirmation and seal.

It can be seen, then, that Nietzsche's psychological test can stimulate wide-ranging reflection. It also provides an alternative way of seeing some of the concerns that are the subject of this book. Asking a question such as 'Can you affirm the eternal recurrence of a world where people are and continue to be seriously deprived?' can trigger personal reflection of a nature that is distinct from the more abstract considerations hitherto presented. Indeed, it may provide us with some motivational zest. The strength of Nietzsche's test lies in its ability to make the plight of others intrinsic to the evaluation of one's own life. Even if one is happy about one's own life, one might not be able to affirm the recurrence of the circumstances both in which it has arisen and in which it is now situated. One might not be able to affirm, for example, the repetition of one's own rather contented existence in a prosperous world where some people continue to have little choice but to sleep under damp cardboard in shop doorways. In this way, concerns of social justice are rendered more immediate and personal. They are bound up with an appraisal of our own lives. If we cannot affirm the recurrence of a prosperous world where some continue to have little choice but to sleep under damp cardboard in shop doorways, then, according to Nietzsche, we cannot coherently affirm the recurrence of our own lives. Moreover, the thought of eternal recurrence arrests us to the important fact that we can at least do something about the circumstances in which our lives and the lives of others *continue*. So, if Nietzsche's test has the desired effect on us, it might motivate us to do something for those less fortunate than ourselves so as to make the world and, by implication, our own existence, something that can be more readily affirmed.

Detwiler worries that such a thought experiment is at best unrealistic, that the Dionysian affirmation that is required to respond positively to Nietzsche's test does not amount to affirmation of life as it really is. He asserts that Nietzsche is unable to affirm the life of this world except in those rare instances where its embodiments approach perfection and asks, 'should the quiet joys and daily triumphs of ordinary people living ordinary lives count for nothing as an ultimate end?'[31] If nobody could respond positively to the idea of eternal recurrence apart from a handful of Nietzscheans, we might justly be alarmed. The test would, by implication, devalue human life. This is far from Nietzsche's aim. He is merely articulating what he thinks it is to face up to and affirm the life of this world and encouraging us to think about what doing so might require. This by no means precludes anyone from affirming the life of this world, although I have suggested that we might have more courage to do so if we made it a more congenial place. Indeed, that many would not have such courage is what motivates Nietzsche's experiment, for he feels that it is they who are devaluing their own lives and the world in which they are situated. What Nietzsche makes clear is that our future, our future situation and our future evaluations thereof are very much in our own hands. He thinks that knowledge should change us.

Another objection to Nietzsche's idea of eternal recurrence is that it fails to rule out enough. It requires that we crave nothing more fervently than to live our life in this world innumerable times more, but says nothing with regard to what that life should be like. Consequently, it is held that the idea cannot amount to a heavy ethical burden since a morally repulsive person could respond positively to it. Nehamas writes that:

> Nietzsche is clearly much more concerned with the question of how one's actions fit together into a coherent, self-sustaining, well motivated whole than he is with the quality of those actions themselves ... the uncomfortable feeling persists that someone might achieve Nietzsche's ideal life and still be nothing short of repugnant.'[32]

Nietzsche is anxious not to prescribe 'the way' through his doctrine of eternal recurrence: 'This – is now my way: where is yours? Thus I answered those who asked me "the way". For the way – does not exist!'[33] However, Nietzsche must to some extent value the affirmation of human life since his doctrine of eternal recurrence remonstrates against its devaluation. We might thereby infer that measures such as provision for conditional basic freedoms that assist the living of life in any 'way' at all would be held to be a good thing.[34] We can at least assume that Nietzsche holds the affirmation of life as it is in this world to be a good thing. Otherwise, to 'desire this once more and innumerable times more' could not be held to be an 'ultimate confirmation and seal'. As Clark ably puts it, 'this ideal tells us not what all of our values should be, but only that whatever they are, they should be rooted in service to life rather than resentment against it.'[35] So, we can hardly regard 'do unto others as you would do to them innumerable times over' as a fitting test of moral aptitude. It is not Nietzsche's style to make heavy ethical prescriptions. We can infer, however, that measures rooted in service to life can only assist its affirmation. Moreover, there is no reason why Nietzsche's strong emphasis on individual self-affirmation cannot be tethered to or, indeed, be essentially bound up with a concern for others.

Nietzsche's Zarathustra upholds truthfulness as the supreme virtue.[36] The idea of eternal recurrence implores us to truthfully face up to the reality of our lives and this world. It has been suggested that it is not, as is often supposed, a crude cosmology, but a certain kind of thought experiment. It amounts to a test as to what our reaction would be to the thought of being psychologically continuous with the repetition of our selfsame life in this selfsame world. Such a test can be seen to be insensitive to the tragedies and atrocities endemic in human life. However, we have seen that this is the main point of the idea of eternal recurrence. The idea of unreservedly affirming the eternal recurrence of the whole world amounts to an enormously heavy burden. If we cannot affirm our world with, amongst other things, its radical inequality of human freedom, then we cannot coherently affirm our own lives. Such an idea thereby implores us to consider how we can become better disposed both to the world and to our own lives.

Nietzsche's test draws our attention to the fact that, even if we have profound regrets up to now or simply do not like some aspects of the world in which we live very much, we can at least work to do something about the circumstances in which our lives and the lives of others continue. In this way, such reflection comes to the assistance of the more abstract arguments discussed in earlier chapters. The reasons hitherto presented as to why we should provide in cases of social deprivation are both augmented and animated by attending to the test of eternal recurrence. It makes us think about what we can (re)live with and, by implication, what we might like to change. Likewise, considerations of social justice are made more immediate and personally pressing because the plight of others is made intrinsic to the evaluation of our own lives by Nietzsche. As such, we are further encouraged to not continue to ignore them.

# 11 The role of genealogy

If we are unhappy about the world, then Nietzsche's test of eternal recurrence implores us to do something about it. If we continue not to do anything, then we cannot coherently affirm our own lives. That we might not be too happy is elaborated upon henceforth. Nietzsche's genealogy adds descriptive colour to our theoretical investigation. Although the style of his genealogy is unbecoming of philosophical ethics, it is arguable that a lot can be achieved by attending to a genealogy of morals such as Nietzsche's. It offers both a reinterpretation of our moral ancestry and a re-evaluation of our present morality system. Specific reference will be made here to his writing on suffering, given that this whole enquiry is in great part motivated by concern about the continuation of remediable human hardship. Nietzsche's imaginative historical and psychological insights provide a very different account of how our morality system copes with human suffering. They enrich our understanding of human hardship, sensitising us to its density and uniqueness. The more we appreciate the dynamics of human hardship, the more we should be motivated to do something about specific instances of human hardship, namely, social deprivations. In so far as genealogy facilitates such appreciation, it is a valuable asset both to our present enquiry and to philosophical enquiry more generally.

The first thing to note about Nietzsche's genealogy of morals is that it is not simply genealogy understood as tracing a pedigree. Nietzsche is not interested in discovering origins of morality when they are seen as an obvious or natural place that can be designated 'the origin' and where enquiry can stop.[1] Rather, he emphasises separate series of processes, his project being to disentangle the synthesis of meanings that have crystallised through the course of history.[2]

Moreover, Nietzsche is anxious to reject the idea that 'things are most precious and essential at the moment of birth'. The assumption that we would approve of our origins is a tacit assumption of much historiography and constitutes an obstacle to our understanding.[3] For Nietzsche, such an assumption is plainly false: the beginnings of everything great on earth were 'soaked in blood thoroughly and for a long time.'[4] So, genealogy should not 'awaken the feeling of man's sovereignty by showing his divine birth: this path is now forbidden, since a monkey stands at the entrance.'[5]

It is not so much that genealogy is thereby distinct from or opposed to history, but rather that Nietzsche supposes it to be more rigorous and accurate than traditional history. As Nehamas notes, Nietzsche insists that genealogy simply is history, correctly practised.[6] It would be misleading, however, to assume that Nietzsche's history is thereby dutifully concerned with and more accurate with respect to origins, dates, places, people and events in history. Rather, his genealogy is more prone to quasi-mythological reconstruction, psychological speculation and creative literary interpretation.[7] It is these aspects of Nietzsche's genealogy that evoke so much that is of interest to philosophical enquiry.

Bernard Williams asserts that a Nietzschean genealogy 'typically combines, in a way that analytical philosophy finds embarrassing, history, phenomenology, "realistic" psychology, and conceptual interpretation'.[8] Nietzsche's historical stories are provocative reinterpretations of the history of morality, which serve to question our conventional understanding. They are further designed to question the propriety of our morality system. These are two different things. As Nietzsche notes, 'Even if a morality has grown out of an error, the realisation of this fact would not as much as touch the problem of its value.'[9] Thus, although Nietzsche is aware of the dangers of occasioning an egregious instance of the genetic fallacy, he wants to examine and question the value of 'that most famous of all medicines which is called morality' and it is difficult to separate this enterprise from his genealogy. This is because, for Nietzsche, the genealogy of morals supports the psychological diagnoses and cultural criticisms that he wishes to make. Genealogy is Nietzsche's springboard, which gives rise to a difficulty in divorcing interpretation from evaluation. 'Many of the book's confusions are attributable to Nietzsche's failure (or unwillingness) to distinguish clearly between his genealogy of morals and the critical method it enables.'[10]

Methodological confusions aside, a Nietzschean genealogy of morals evokes much that is of interest to philosophical enquiry. MacIntyre argues that the task of Nietzsche's genealogy of morals was to 'exhibit the historical genesis of the psychological deformation involved in the morality of the late nineteenth century and the philosophy and theology which sustained it'.[11] Of grave concern to Nietzsche, among other things, was how human beings cope with suffering and this section will illustrate how his psychological insight, historical conjecture and subsequent discussions thereof contribute to our understanding of suffering. Although this will by no means exhaust the content of Nietzsche's genealogy, it will vindicate this sort of method and show how it might be put to good use. Such understanding, in turn, can only assist our present enquiry.

'The problem of the value of pity and the morality of pity'[12] is a fundamental concern for Nietzsche. In order to question the 'value of these values' Nietzsche asserts that we need 'a knowledge of the conditions in which they grew, under which they evolved and changed'.[13] According to Nietzsche, these values come about through our 'mortal hatred for suffering', as a response to pain.

> For every sufferer instinctively seeks a cause for his suffering; more exactly, an agent; still more specifically, a guilty agent who is susceptible to suffering – in short, some living thing upon which he can, on some pretext or other, vent his affects, actually or in effigy: for the venting of his affects represents the greatest attempt on the part of the suffering to win relief, anaesthesia – the narcotic he cannot help desiring to deaden pain of any kind. This alone, I surmise, constitutes the actual physiological cause of ressentiment, vengefulness, and the like: a desire to deaden pain by means of affects.[14]

Morality thus evolves for Nietzsche from the need of human beings to cope with their suffering. Morality gives suffering a meaning, that meaning being all important to its relief. Indeed, Nietzsche argues that it is not suffering itself that human beings cannot cope with, but meaningless suffering. They 'do not repudiate suffering as such; they desire it, they even seek it out, provided they are shown a meaning for it, a purpose of suffering'.[15]

Without morality, then, human suffering receives no anaesthesia; it remains meaningless. This is what Nietzsche seems to believe is really the case when he writes about real physiological or social cause as opposed to blaming others.[16] As Nehamas notes, for Nietzsche, 'suffering has no meaning – in itself ... it just stands there, stupid to all eternity'.[17] It is morality that imposes meaning on suffering, so as to make it tolerable.

What interests Nietzsche is the particular way in which morality gives meaning to suffering, that is, the kinds of reasons offered to relieve suffering and the effects thereof. He locates the genesis of such reasons with the ascetic priest:

> "I suffer: someone must be to blame for it" – thus thinks every sickly sheep. But his shepherd, the ascetic priest, tells him: "Quite so my sheep! Someone must be to blame for it: but you yourself are this someone, you alone are to blame for it – you alone are to blame for yourself!"[18]

The effect of this 'brazen and false enough' claim according to Nietzsche is that the 'direction of ressentiment is altered'.

> Man, suffering from himself in some way or other ... receives a hint, he receives from his sorcerer, the ascetic priest, the first hint as to the "cause" of his suffering: he must seek it in himself, in some guilt, in a piece of the past, he must understand his suffering as a punishment ... the invalid has been transformed into "the sinner".[19]

That transformation, for Nietzsche, heralds the birth of the 'morality of pity'.

Giving suffering a meaning as punishment for sin offers man a remedy. The 'sickly sheep' transform their suffering into the cornerstone for a new brand of morality whereby they 'announce that they deserve to suffer, and that they therefore prefer humility and submission to the apparent prosperity of the nobles'.[20] Man erects an ideal, that of a 'holy god', and feels in the face of it the palpable certainty of his own absolute unworthiness.[21] The problem for Nietzsche is that he believes that this is the wrong meaning to attach to human suffering. He finds it opposed to nature, a wrong road where both self deception and further suffering can be the only destination.

Nietzsche argues that the morality of pity, the moralisation of the concepts of guilt and duty, amounts to a repression of our animal instincts.

> You will have guessed what has really happened here, beneath all this: that will to self-tormenting, that repressed cruelty of the animal made inward ... who invented the bad conscience in order to hurt himself after the more natural vent for this desire to hurt had been blocked ... He apprehends in "God" the ultimate antithesis of his own ineluctable animal instincts; he reinterprets these animal instincts themselves as a form of guilt before God (as hostility, rebellion, insurrection against the "Lord", the "father", the primal ancestor and origin of the world).[22]

It follows from this that the only way to reduce our suffering is to refrain from doing that which morality deems to be responsible for it. For Nietzsche, this entails having to deny our instincts and this sort of 'ascetic self-flagellation' is clearly inhuman according to him. The repression of our animal instincts amounts to a denial of life:

> this hatred of the human, and even more of the animal, and more still of the material, this horror of the senses, of reason itself, this fear of happiness and beauty, this longing to get away from all appearance, change, becoming, death, wishing, from longing itself – all this means – let us dare to grasp it – *a will to nothingness*, an aversion to life, a rebellion against the most fundamental presuppositions of life. [23]

The interpretation of human suffering offered by the morality of pity will thus, according to Nietzsche, bring 'fresh suffering with it, deeper, more inward, more poisonous, more life-destructive suffering'.[24] It is consequently the wrong reaction; 'the treatment it prescribes is deadlier than the condition it purports to treat'.[25]

Nietzsche's historical story has, so far, identified a psychological need in human beings to cope with suffering resulting in the creation of a morality, which, according to Nietzsche, will perpetuate human suffering. Christian morality is the wrong reaction for Nietzsche precisely because it is a reaction. Nietzsche writes about our 'incapacity to remain spectators of suffering, to let suffer'.[26] Our moral construction is an attempt to abolish suffering with the result that we are diminishing ourselves.[27] This has further ramifications for Nietzsche with respect to both our comprehension of suffering and our acknowledgement of individuality.

Nietzsche argues that 'our personal and profoundest suffering is incomprehensible and inaccessible to almost everyone ... one simply knows nothing of the whole inner sequence and intricacies that are distress for *me* or for *you*'.[28] This is ignored by the morality of pity:

> whenever people notice that we suffer, they interpret our suffering superficially ... all such things that may be involved in distress are of no concern to our dear pitying friends; they wish to help ... and they believe that they have helped most when they have helped most quickly.[29]

As a result, for Nietzsche, our morality demeans suffering and the sufferer. Havas observes that, 'Rather than letting the sufferer suffer, the pitier insists on eliminating his suffering, on calming him. Pity refuses to let him speak.'[30]

Nietzsche is contending that our morality system constitutes a failure to listen to the sufferer. It is a superficial reaction to suffering that does not face up to it. We are failing to understand the full profundity of suffering through our silencing of the individual. As such, the morality of pity is said to be 'hostile to the very possibility of individuality'.[31]

Nietzsche's genealogy, then, not only perceives our morality as an inadequate life-denying response to human suffering, but perceives it as a response that perpetuates and is based on an impoverished articulation of that suffering. We deny the voluptuousness of our own experiences through the immediate dismissal of suffering and displeasure as 'evil, hateful, worthy of annihilation, and as a defect of existence'.[32] Nietzsche argues that to continue to live under such a morality will be to ensure that we 'remain small together'.[33]

Nietzsche's imaginative reinterpretation encourages reflection about human suffering. He is urging us to consider the idea that, historically, we have coped with suffering in the wrong way. We have reacted to it *prior to its comprehension* with the result that we have denied life and deceived ourselves. Havas argues that the goal of the genealogy is to provide the kind of memory that enables us to realise this[34] and therefore to do something about it. The self-consciousness afforded by an honest understanding of human history will allow us to make something out of our suffering and thereby give it a meaning in the service of life rather than in the service of psychological deformation.[35] If we were to deny here that anything was achieved by the genealogy of morals, we could be said to be failing to listen to the sufferer. Indeed, philosophical enquiry might draw a lot from this kind of creative psychological analysis.

Although much of what Nietzsche says here may seem perfectly irrelevant to the subject at hand, we do not have to accept the truth or relevance of his whole story to benefit from the insights contained within it. Indeed, Nietzsche provides an alternative source of general understanding that can be seen to have specific application. That is to say, any assistance in understanding the dynamics of human hardship must in turn contribute to an appreciation of the gravity and uniqueness of particular examples of it. In this way, Nietzsche's rich narrative can enlighten us about the emotional complexity and density of experiences bound up with social deprivation. His analysis highlights a depth of feeling – a voluptuousness – that can be missed by abstract theoretical consideration of deprivation and hardship. It should, by implication, inform and enrich our enquiry.

Nietzsche implores us to listen to others and to acknowledge the profundity of what they go through. For example, the worst thing that we could say to Mrs Smith about her deep regret and her struggle with ill health would be, according to Nietzsche, 'I know how you feel'. On his account, we clearly cannot fully know just how Mrs Smith feels. We cannot fully comprehend the intricacies and depths of her experiences, nor should we purport to. To say that we know how she feels is likely to close off her conversation (if we know how she feels, there is no need for her to continue to tell us!) and, in so doing, is dismissive of the uniqueness of her person. Likewise, these kinds of observations recommend that we should not be dismissive of those who experience social deprivation. For example, we cannot know just how it feels for a particular person to sleep rough day after day, to be looked upon as a parasite, to not see any brightness at all in their future or to be considered unfit for marriage. Nor can we know how it feels for a particular person to struggle to get about their environment, to be manhandled up steps, to be discriminated against or to feel trapped inside their own body or mind. Nietzsche's genealogy arrests us to the uniqueness and complexity of other people's experiences and urges that we cease to silence or demean them. It lends texture to our comprehension of particular realities – realities that in many cases we can do an awful lot about. In so far as it does this, Nietzsche's contribution should make those realities harder to dismiss. Correspondingly, it is an asset to the process of trying to motivate social and political change. That is to say, the more we acknowledge the deeply personal and person affecting nature of the experiences that tend to be associated with enduring social deprivations, the more likely it is that we will be inclined to do something about those deprivations.

Focussing on the voluptuousness and individuality of human experience, then, might entail that we become a little more sensitive and compassionate with respect to the very real challenges that people presently have to live with. Nietzsche quite usefully reminds us (in a variety of ways) about human vulnerability, which can be forgotten or obscured at times both in theory and in practice. It might be beneficial to keep that reminder at the forefront of considerations about future social and economic policies. Moreover, Nietzsche warns us against feeling that we have helped others most when we have helped them most quickly. That alerts us to the importance of looking at incidents of human hardship such as the deprivation of freedom considerately and, necessarily, at the expense of brevity. This is something that could also be said to be critical to thinking appropriately about issues like social deprivation. In addition, we can put Nietzsche's literary remonstration against an aversion to life to serious use.[36] It can be used to support the recommendation that we should not uphold both a morality system in general and the conditions of our society in particular, where it is tolerable that some people continue to face undeserved and unnecessary impediments to their pursuit of basic freedoms and opportunities in life. Granted, some of Nietzsche's ideas are at best irrelevant; yet it has been shown that others inform and animate the subject of our philosophical enquiry. We should not ignore that creative and provocative input.

Just how much can be achieved by attending to a Nietzschean genealogy of morals is of course a different question. A Nietzschean genealogy brings with it its own problems. His style and method does not sit comfortably with analytical philosophy and the question of what status can be coherently accorded to his claims within his philosophy more generally is hotly debated.[37] Yet what has been illustrated via discussion of Nietzsche's consideration of human hardship is that he can be put to 'serious use'. 'One serious use is to help us with issues that press on any serious philosophy (in particular, moral philosophy) that does not beg the most basic of its own questions.'[38] This is not to argue that *everything* can be achieved by attending to a genealogy of morals such as Nietzsche's. Indeed, to deny the propriety of other styles of thought and other sources of understanding would be as misguided as denying the propriety of some of Nietzsche's reflections.

Therefore, if we refrain from thinking of achievement or lack thereof as depending upon whether or not we accept Nietzsche's genealogy at the expense of other styles of thought and other sources of understanding, we can assert that, at the very least, the genealogy of morals makes a positive contribution to our philosophical enquiry. It should not be seen as being opposed to that enquiry but rather as comprising a valuable part of it. Nietzsche's provocations are only unhelpful if we find his style unsettling or want to resist imaginative conjecture. That would seem to amount to a rather restricted approach. Moreover, it is clearly not Nietzsche's intention to obstruct the progress of or damage philosophical enquiry. He hopes for a 'man who justifies man'[39] who may one day 'bring home the redemption of this reality'.[40] This requires, for Nietzsche, that we become intelligible to ourselves through an appropriate understanding of the past. The purpose of his genealogy is to free the horizon – to help rather than hinder the progression of philosophical enquiry.

Having discussed Nietzsche's creative historical interpretation and psychological insight with regard to human hardship, it must be noted that there is far more to his genealogy than has been touched upon here. Moreover, as has been previously intimated, some of Nietzsche's procedures are certainly less helpful than others.[41] We may rightly be, then, more than a little selective in our use of Nietzsche's ideas. Heeding Nietzsche's warning against writing history through the distorting lens of one's own moral convictions does not, for example, entail embracing his 'own peculiar conception of individualism'.[42] Similarly, Nietzsche's interpretation of the moralisation of the concepts of guilt and duty and the resulting conception of blame as originating in the sentiment of ressentiment requires additional interpretation that attends to, for example, the idea of fairness.[43]

However, the aspects of Nietzsche's thought that are less helpful than others still contribute to the progress of philosophical enquiry in so far as they challenge us, even if only in a way that consolidates our reasons for rejecting them. That they are less helpful points to the fact that there is room for improvement to Nietzsche's reinterpretation of our moral ancestry and to his re-evaluation of our morality system. It does not point to the fact that Nietzsche's project was mistaken. Indeed, as Williams argues, we need such elements as history, phenomenology, realistic psychology and conceptual interpretation to work together:

> We need to understand what parts of our conceptual scheme are, in what degree, culturally local. We understand this best when we understand an actual human scheme that differs from ours in certain respects. One, very important, way of locating such a scheme is finding it in history, in particular in the history of our own scheme. In order to understand that other scheme, and to understand why there should be this difference between those people and ourselves, we need to understand it as a human scheme; this is to understand the differences in terms of similarities, which calls on psychological interpretation.[44]

The eclecticism that gained expression in Nietzsche's writing can be seen, then, to be of considerable use to philosophical enquiry. If philosophy is isolated from other disciplines then, in turn, it will be isolated from different sources of understanding. It is hard to see how that could be at all helpful.

Nietzsche's discussion of human suffering shows how his genealogy of morals can stimulate reflection that enriches our understanding of ourselves and others. In so far as philosophical enquiry aims at a better understanding of human beings, it should therefore be similarly enriched. It has also been suggested that, more specifically, Nietzsche's genealogy can contribute to a better awareness of the uniqueness and profundity of people's experiences of social deprivations. It should thereby heighten our concern about those deprivations and, in turn, augment the compelling reasons we already have to provide for conditional basic freedoms. More crucially, it might also help to motivate us to *make* that provision.

# 12 Other ways of seeing

In the last chapter we looked at an account of the tendency to interpret human suffering superficially. Elaboration and interpretation about the uniqueness and profundity of human distress reinforced the point that we should not be happy about a world where considerable and remediable human hardship is commonplace and that, indeed, we should do something about it. This chapter looks at other ways of motivating change. The idea will be explored that 'imagination is the chief instrument of the good',[1] that literature and photography, for example, might further sensitise us to the gravity of the deprivations of human freedom being discussed and thereby motivate us to rectify them. The use of these other sources of understanding will be shown, like Nietzsche's genealogy, to be beneficial both to our present project and to philosophical enquiry more generally.

Given the example of Mrs Smith and the proclivity of people to be like her, it has been argued that we should be concerned with supplying some motivational force to compelling philosophical argument. As noted earlier, given that we are considering both a considerable and remediable inequality of human freedom, it is disappointing to think that philosophical arguments presented here and more generally might have very little effect. Indeed, as Posner argues, 'academic moralists who want to alter behaviour, ... ought to worry a lot about how to motivate people to do what they persuade them is the "right" thing to do'.[2] Posner contends that knowing the moral thing to do creates no motivation for doing it and that, even if he is wrong,

> the analytical tools employed in academic moralism – whether moral casuistry, or reasoning from the canonical texts of moral philosophy, or careful analysis, or reflective equilibrium, or some combination of these tools – are too feeble to override either narrow self-interest or moral intuitions.[3]

What we need to do, according to Posner, is to employ rhetorical skill and use factual knowledge: we need to be 'moral entrepreneurs'.[4]

Rorty similarly argues that the motivation to change the way that we treat other people does not come from reflection but is created.

It is created by increasing our sensitivity to the particular details of the pain and humiliation of other, unfamiliar sorts of people. Such increased sensitivity makes it more difficult to marginalize people different from ourselves by thinking, 'They do not feel it as *we* would', or 'There must always be suffering, so why not let *them* suffer?'[5]

He argues that the process of increasing sensitivity is a task best done by 'genres such as ethnography, the journalist's report, the comic book, the docudrama, and, especially, the novel'.[6] Such genres are, he thinks, the 'principal vehicles of moral change and progress'.[7]

The power of genres such as those alluded to by Rorty can certainly be acknowledged in modern society. For example, it was not an academic text, but news reports and television images of dying people that triggered public sympathy for victims of famine in the early eighties, culminating in projects such as 'Live Aid'. Similarly, when we think of the Vietnam War, we tend not to think of outraged ethicists, but instead of the astonishing picture of the naked child running from her village as it was being attacked. In contrast with such sources, analytic philosophical theory is 'unlikely to stir the conscience, incite a sense of indignation, or engender feelings of love or guilt'.[8] This is why charities, for example, 'know that the way to get people to give money for the feeding of starving children is to publish a picture of a starving child, seeking thereby to trigger feelings of sympathy, rather than to talk about a moral duty'.[9] In so far as analytic philosophers are interested in motivating people to change the way that they treat others, then, they should be more than interested in employing alternative resources to give their arguments as much motivational force as they can.

At this juncture, then, it might be effective, if technology permitted, to project moving images of a person with hopelessness in their eyes, struggling to stay warm on a bleak wintry night under an assortment of crumpled newspapers. We could project images too, of a lone child in worn-out shoes kicking a deflated ball around a desolate concrete square. A soundtrack of Saint-Saëns 'Calme des nuits' or Garbarek's version of Grieg's 'Arietta' might further trigger feelings of sadness. Similarly, if given the chance, we might have got through to Mrs Smith not by reasoning with her, but by relating stories of her daughter's grief or by playing her a video of her grandchild at play. Rorty endorses such tactics. When answering the question of why we should care about strangers, for example, he recommends

the sort of long, sad, sentimental story which begins 'Because this is what it is like to be in her situation – to be far from home, among strangers,' or 'Because she might become your daughter-in-law,' or 'Because her mother would grieve for her.'[10]

If such tactics supply motivational force to philosophical theory, then, there would seem to be good reason to employ them. However, it is also important to realise the potential pitfalls of appealing to sentiment. That there are some is not always appreciated.

While the appeal to sentiment is endorsed as being catalytic to moral change by writers such as Rorty and Posner, the role of theory tends to be correspondingly repudiated.[11] This is neither inevitable nor desirable. That is to say, it is perfectly legitimate to argue that other sources of under-standing are more motivationally effective than theory without undermining the importance and necessity of theory to any progressive philosophical enquiry. Indeed, without good theory, an appeal to sentiment could lead to actions that are misguided or, most certainly, inappropriate given other choices.

Appeal to sentiment with bad, little or no theoretical underpinning might very well lead us in the wrong direction. For example, after endless exposure to sentimental television programmes about animals, we might find ourselves motivated to do some rather extraordinary things. This is evidenced by stories of people who have jumped into freezing cold water and put their lives at risk to save a distressed puppy, or people who have not waited for the fire brigade before trying to rescue a kitten from the top of a tree. The sentiments acted upon here could be said to be highly disproportionate to the reasons so to act. The saving of the life of a young dog or cat, while admirable, might not be said to be at all worth risking the immeasurable grief of one's husband or wife, for example, or son or daughter, or sister or brother. These sorts of actions could therefore be said to be, at the very least, misguided. Likewise, an appeal to sentiment could lead us to get our priorities wrong. We could find ourselves, for example, being inclined to rescue pets *before* we were inclined to rescue people.[12] So, in the interests of not acting in a misguided or inappropriate way, an appeal to sentiment needs a sound theoretical basis. That basis informs us both when there is good reason to appeal to sentiment to try to motivate action and where our priorities with regard to potential action should lie.

There is no reason, then, why alternative methods of motivation and philosophical theory should not sit quite cheerfully together. Indeed, the more of a match there is between the use of a motivational tactic and the reasons we have to use it, the better. With that in mind, it is not controversial to suggest that, in so far as provision in cases of social deprivation is more rationally defensible than, for example, supplying wetsuits to people so that they are equipped to rescue distressed puppies from freezing lakes, or funding veterinary practices to enable overweight hamsters to have heart bypass operations, the use of other sources to encourage that we make that provision must be similarly more defensible. To deny a role for theory would be as mistaken as denying that alternative sources of understanding and motivation can be put to good use. It would be rather like adding attractive trim and a turbocharger to a car while removing its engine and steering wheel.

As well as grounding alternative sources of motivation that appeal to sentiment in reason, it is important to appeal to sentiment that is appropriate to the subject at hand. Otherwise, the use of other ways of seeing could be counter-productive. It could be said, for example, that much of the problem faced by people with impairments and a great part of the reason why disability issues have not been considered to be issues of social justice, is the continued dominance of less helpful sentiments such as pity and charity. Similarly, evoking sentiments such as pity with regard to people who are homeless can be taken to imply that such people should be grateful[13] for a cup of watery soup. Now in so far as any theory of social justice arguing for the provision of conditional basic freedoms for all should have no room for the above sentiments, it should be careful to avoid evoking them. Our task instead should be to evoke sympathy for others and to sensitise people to their particular situations in a way that is not condescending. We might even try to provoke embarrassment at the fact that societies can fail some of their members so miserably. That aside, it is wise that the theoretician be aware of the potential counter-productivity of appealing to sentiment.[14]

Another potential problem with regard to the use of sources that appeal to sentiment is diminishing effectiveness due to overexposure. That is to say, the power of appeals to sentiment is to a large extent dependent on audience susceptibility and this can dwindle through overload. Overexposure can breed immunity. So, for example, even appeals to sentiment that have had astounding results, such as 'Comic Relief' and 'Children in Need', tend to raise less money the more frequently their appeals are repeated. While we might find that disturbing, it recommends that appeals to sentiment be used sparingly so that they retain their potency. The theorist as tactician should avoid 'flooding the market', then, so that alternative sources of understanding do not become 'just another sad story', 'just another disturbing photograph' or 'just another harrowing news report', because then they would lose much of their power and, by implication, cease to augment reason.[15]

So far, it has been argued that, in as much as analytic philosophers are interested in motivating people to change the way that they treat others, they have good reason to employ alternative sources so as to give their arguments more motivational force. If they do so, they should be careful to appeal to the appropriate sentiment. They should also beware of creating an immunity to sensitising sources. Moreover, the employment of alternative motivational sources should not be at the expense of theory. The more grounded in reason an appeal to sentiment is, the more justified that appeal is likely to be. That said, there are compelling reasons to provide in cases of social deprivation. Correspondingly, there are compelling reasons to use other ways of seeing to try to motivate people to make that provision. Henceforth, some alternative sources that might augment our reasons to provide for conditional basic freedoms will be presented. First, however, the other side of the rhetorical coin must be attended to.

## Libertarianism on stilts

We saw in Chapter 11 that Nietzsche remonstrates against the idea that people in some way deserve to suffer. In attempting to extinguish the religious basis for such an idea, however, he leaves room for an atheistic argument to the same effect. Writers such as Joseph, Sumption and Boyson can be seen to support such a position. Their rhetoric appeals to sentiments that are diametrically opposed to those that anyone sympathetic to the arguments so far would try to evoke. While such literature might seem incredible, it is only thorough to deal with it.

The idea appealed to by writers such as Joseph, Sumption and Boyson is that people who are relatively socially deprived are little more than envious parasites. According to Joseph and Sumption, inequalities of income and all that they entail merely reflect the fact that some people are more useful than others,[16] and it is predictable that people will resent 'those whose achievements have emphasised their own timidity'.[17] The idea of redistributing income so as to provide freedoms for those people is thereby repugnant.

> There is no greater tyranny possible than denying to individuals the disposal of their own talents. When this is done for no other reason than that the talents are resented by those who do not have, do not use or do not like them, the result is not only economically wasteful and morally indefensible, but destructive of the spirit of large tolerance on which any open society must be based.[18]

It follows from this that we should avoid creating a society where 'the state spends all its energies taking money from the energetic, successful and thrifty to give it to the idle, the failures and the feckless'.[19] Indeed, such a society, in contrast with capitalist societies, will inevitably be characterised by 'show trials, concentration camps, mass murder, the use of mental asylums to punish dissent, "cultural revolution", conscription of labour and xenophobia'.[20] Redistribution, then, is both 'misconceived in theory and repellent in practice'; we should just get used to the fact that there are some people 'whose lot it is to be poor'.[21]

The above rhetoric, taken seriously, could be rather surprising, if not frightening, to anybody sympathetic to the idea of redistribution. Moreover, Joseph and Sumption argue that to disagree with them amounts to supporting the proposition that our free choices in a free society must be 'evil'. 'Since inequality arises from the operation of innumerable individual preferences it cannot be evil unless those preferences are themselves evil.'[22] As Haworth points out, this claim is clearly false:

> consider: for reasons of personal hygiene, millions of individuals spray themselves with a small amount of underarm deodorant each morning. As a result, the ozone layer develops a hole, the globe warms up, polar

ice-caps start to melt, and the demise of the human race starts to look a distinct possibility. Sir Keith Joseph thinks that an outcome can be evil only if the preferences which give rise to it are evil, so is he against personal hygiene or in favour of the demise of the human race? It's hard to believe that he is really either.[23]

Thus, Joseph and Sumption's argument does not stand up to logical analysis. However, that is not the most important point here.[24] Rather, the main worry about the above passages is that they could have considerable rhetorical power. They imply that we are *weak* and *resentful* if we want to *take* from those more successful than ourselves, that going down such a road can only lead to *totalitarianism* and that to argue otherwise is to argue that our own market preferences are *evil*. Such words disguise the issues while they both insult our sympathies and equate acting upon them with social catastrophe. It is reasonable to assume that they could also be powerful enough in some contexts to persuade, delude or frighten people to a sufficient degree to deter support for social provision. Tactics such as these, then, can lead people to acquiesce in the endurance of conditions detrimental to their freedom.[25]

The existence of passages such as those cited above reinforces the need both for the theoretical investigation of preceding chapters and for powerful counter-rhetoric. The implications of such passages need to be exposed. For example, even if it were the case that people in some way deserved to be socially deprived,[26] to suggest that we should fail to do anything about the considerable hardships experienced by others is not far short of sadistic. With regard to that sort of suggestion, Orwell writes, 'I often wonder whether that kind of stuff deceives even the fools who utter it'.[27] The passages below encourage reflection of a rather different kind.

## Alternative perspectives

On the subject of motivating people to do something about remediable human hardship, Orwell ruminates 'if only one could find the word that would move them'.[28] The following literature attempts to do this. Its focus is on homelessness in particular[29] and on relative social deprivation more generally. Attention to that literature will expose the callousness of the rhetorical capitalist, further sensitise us to the gravity of some of the deprivations of human freedom being discussed and, by implication, assist in motivating us to do something about them.

Contrary to what Joseph and others would have us believe, 'one cannot imagine the average Englishman deliberately turning parasite'.[30] Indeed, a homeless man is

> only an Englishman out of work ... I am not saying, of course, that most
> tramps are ideal characters; I am only saying that they are ordinary

human beings, and that if they are worse than other people it is the result and not the cause of their way of life.[31]

The testimony of Tony Wilkinson bears this out: a reporter living on the streets of London for a month, he found the response to the change of his appearance astonishing.

> By late afternoon the contempt from passers-by began to depress me considerably. It was no use telling myself that I did not deserve such looks of loathing, and that my personality was still intact under the dirty surface. Knowing that I had weeks of such contumely to follow, I began to hate the person I had become for visiting hatred upon me. It was his fault I was despised, his fault I was denied human warmth, and I wanted to murder him then and there. If only I could tell people who I really was, I thought, they would understand. But there was no way I could approach people. I felt a pressure to conform as strong as anything I had experienced since being a teenager, the claustrophobic feeling that acceptability was only a change of clothes away ... I tried to say: I am human like you. But my appearance only succeeded in communicating: danger, do not approach.[32]

It is important to remember, then, that the subject of this academic enquiry is, at root, human beings. As was noted in the last chapter, sight of this can be lost through the lens of abstract philosophical theory. The idea that their subject has feelings seems especially lost on libertarians like Joseph and Sumption. Berger's story about homeless people acts as a further reminder. Consider, for example, his description of a homeless couple, Vico and Vica, and their dog who is narrator.

> One of the things the three of us agree about is sleep. I'm not sure which of us sleeps more lightly. Maybe we sleep deeply in turns. Sometimes I sleep on his side, sometimes on hers. I always sleep with them and I never sleep between them. When we are asleep, the three of us together, we are protected ... Our agreement that sleep is best, and the fact that we are three, lets our bodies relax after we've lain down.
>      When it's freezing and there's nothing to burn, which is often the case, they go to bed fully dressed and wearing gloves. Before they go to sleep each takes off a glove to hold the other's hand for a moment.[33]

Sentences such as these and 'Vico can't scavenge. He's still afraid his mother will see him',[34] or 'He looked at the edge of his toast as if it were the only friend he had in the world',[35] make vivid to us both the humanity of people who are homeless and some of the realities bound up with homelessness. It is easy to remain unaware of the fact, for example, that homelessness generally entails being cut off from the prospect of finding a partner. 'Few couples survive the calamity as a couple. The sight of the other makes things worse for them.'[36] Moreover, if one is single, a single male in this extract:

> it goes without saying that if (he) finds no women at his own level, those above – even a very little above – are as far out of reach as the moon... women never, or hardly ever, condescend to men who are much poorer than themselves. A tramp, therefore, is a celibate from the moment when he takes to the road. He is absolutely without hope of getting a wife.[37]

Along similar lines, Wilkinson describes two women passing by his park bench. 'I smiled, and they quickened their pace. So that was another loss I would have to come to terms with, I thought – my loss of sexuality.'[38] The ramifications of such a loss are profound according to Orwell:

> there is the degradation worked in a man who knows he is not even considered fit for marriage. The evil of poverty is not so much that it makes a man suffer as that it rots him physically and spiritually. And there can be no doubt that sexual starvation contributes to this rotting process ... No humiliation could do more damage to a man's self respect.[39]

In addition, it is worth attending to description of the experience of hunger that can be bound up with serious relative social deprivation. Consider, for example, Orwell's description of the second day that he had gone without food:

> I thought of pawning my overcoat, but it seemed too far to walk to the pawnshop, and I spent the day in bed, reading the *Memoirs of Sherlock Holmes*. It was all that I felt equal to, without food. Hunger reduces one to an utterly spineless, brainless condition, more like the after-effects of influenza than anything else. It is as though one had been turned into a jellyfish, or as though all one's blood had been pumped out and lukewarm water substituted.[40]

While experience of hunger to this degree could be said to be rare, the experience of being condemned as 'the idle, the failures and the feckless' is not. Wilkinson describes his experience of being despised on the streets: 'I felt people were willing me to step off the pavement to let them pass. They walked round me as if they were avoiding dog faeces.'[41] Berger's dog elaborates:

> The sidewalk is wide and many people pass. At the moment about twenty people are passing a minute. That's to say about nineteen times a minute Vico and I are rubbed out, not seen. ...

> The hatred which the strong feel for the weak as soon as the weak get too close is particularly human; it doesn't happen with animals. With

humans there is a distance which must be respected, and when it isn't, it is the strong, not the weak, who feel affronted, and from the affront comes hatred.[42]

It is hard to imagine what it must feel like to be 'rubbed out, not seen'. Indeed, perhaps we are likely to be more familiar with how it is to feel affronted. It is also worth thinking about the physical discomfort that serious relative social deprivation can entail. For example, 'it is worth remembering that the average tramp has no clothes but what he stands up in, wears boots that are ill-fitting, and does not sit in a chair for months together'.[43] Even if we have experienced the discomfort of sleeping on a floor, that experience is generally followed rather quickly by a euphoric reunification with a sprung mattress and a goose-down duvet. Sleeping without bedding is altogether different night after night. It is especially different when one is outside.

> I laid out my newspapers, copies of the *Observer*, the *Sunday Times*, the *Guardian* and the *Daily Mail*. On the pavement, they all looked transparently up-market, and I lay on top of them as quickly as I could, before anyone had a chance to notice. I wondered how long it would be before the cold seeped through. I was wearing all the clothes I had set out with, including those in the suitcase. There was a vest, shirt, two pullovers, a car-coat and my thick overcoat. I wore two pairs of trousers, the inner pair tucked into my socks ... the man next to me adjusted his cardboard blanket to cover a part of his back which had been left out in the cold. There was not enough cardboard to cover him fully, and he was forced to make constant readjustments throughout the night.[44]

> The plastic sheet over our pieces of corrugated roofing is weighed down with broken chunks of concrete, but if there's a wind the rain finds its way through and the cardboard ceiling isn't waterproof and starts to drip and the large wet stains grow larger and larger ... the first hopelessness begins when you cannot imagine anything ever being dry again.[45]

Although one might think so, sleeping in a hostel does not seem to amount to much of a marked improvement. Indeed, Wilkinson describes paying for a place in a hostel as paying for 'squalor, danger and neglect; a place where you prayed there would never be a fire'.[46] He also describes a man, typical of what he saw in such hostels, 'doubled up on a dining chair, his head on his knees, like a puppet whose strings had been cut ... stranded like a bottle on a mud bank'.[47]

Much of the despair associated with relative social deprivation comes from the experience of unemployment.

> After disease and premature death, sustained unemployment is one of the worst evils which can befall an ordinary person. In the modern

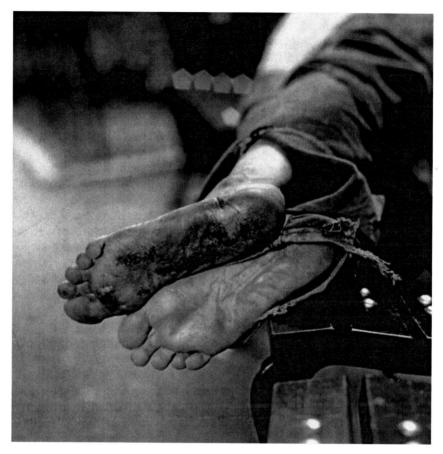

*Figure 12.1*

world, the unemployed person loses more than money. That person loses the ability to plan ahead and to organise his or her life. This can amount to losing the ability to give that life a coherent meaning. It is very likely that he or she will lose a sense of identity, dignity and self-respect as well.[48]

Orwell describes the 'frightful feeling of impotence and despair' tethered to the experience of unemployment, remembering his astonishment at the decency of the unemployed people he met who were 'gazing at their destiny with the same sort of dumb amazement as an animal in a trap'.[49] He remarks that the corroding sense of shame that comes with unemployment is outside the range of his experience.[50] Indeed, much of what has been described above is outside the range of our experience. It is hard to believe that those accounts depict day-to-day experiences of people, today. It is difficult to comprehend, for example, what it must be like when 'suddenly there is no in and no out, and you have to spend the next hour alone, and the next and the next and the next'.[51] It is difficult to comprehend what it must be like to 'go to pieces as you could not possibly do in a place where you had neighbours who knew you'.[52] And it challenges us to acknowledge that the cardboard boxes from which many people joyfully extract consumer good after consumer good have an alternative use as 'temporary housing for the jobless in the capital city of the United Kingdom'.[53]

Deprivation annihilates people's futures, denying them the freedoms that many of us take for granted. The above material makes some of the stark realities of social deprivation immediate to us. It highlights the indecency of the rhetorical capitalist. If any of the above sources move us, then their inclusion here is vindicated, for in as much as they further sensitise us to the deprivations and distresses of others, they might motivate us to act on the compelling reasons that we have to provide in cases of social deprivation. They might disturb us enough to *do* what we can to make sure that people do not remain indifferent to hope, that they do not continue to feel utterly reduced by despair. In short, we might be prompted to stop behaving like Mrs Smith did.

More generally, in so far as analytic philosophers are interested in motivating people to change the way that they treat other people, they should be committed to finding and using alternative sources of understanding to augment their arguments. Indeed, to ignore such sources is to show little respect to those 'who have fought and are fighting the destructive and ignorant trends that are still so powerful, and who have kept the strength to imagine, as well as to work for, human dignity, freedom and peace'.[54]

# Notes

## 1 Relative Social Deprivation

1 B. Shaw, 'Poverty: Absolute or Relative?', 35.
2 See J.D. Jones, *Poverty and the Human Condition: A Philosophical Enquiry*, p.6 and P. Dasgupta, *An Enquiry into Well-being and Destitution*, p. 40.
3 Shaw, 'Poverty: Absolute or Relative?', p. 29.
4 C. Oppenheim, *Poverty: The Facts*, p. 6.
5 Ibid., pp. 7–8.
6 J. MacMahan, 'Cognitive Disability, Misfortune and Justice', 24–5.
7 Church of England, *Faith in the City: A Call For Action by Church and Nation*, p. 195.
8 Dasgupta, *An Enquiry into Well-being* p. 46.
9 Shaw, 'Poverty: Absolute or Relative?', p.35. See also D.S. King and J. Waldron, 'Citizenship, Social Citizenship and the Defence of Welfare Provision', 419.
10 Shaw, 'Poverty: Absolute or Relative?', p. 30.
11 Shaw, 'Poverty: Absolute or Relative?', p. 31.
12 It is far from obvious why we would be at all concerned with relative poverty and thus be motivated to articulate the concept if we were willing to forget the absolute poor once they were 'just above' the subsistence line.
13 I am not alone in using this word. See, for example, J. Scott, *Poverty and Wealth: Citizenship, Deprivation and Privilege*.
14 A drawback with using statistics is that they can become somewhat dated over time. However, the studies cited here together comprise a most comprehensive comparative analysis, containing solid indicators with respect to current deprivation in the UK. Indeed, it is safe to say that, unfortunately, little of note tends to change. For example, in 2006, income support (renamed job seeker's allowance) was set at £56.20 per week for a single person over 25 – just £22.80 more than it was 17 years ago, which is an average increase of £1.34 per year. See http://www.direct.gov.uk.
15 Shaw, 'Poverty: Absolute or Relative?', p. 31.
16 See Dasgupta, *An Enquiry into Well-being*, p. 46 and L.A. Jacobs, *Rights and Deprivation*, p.179. It is worth noting that although a condition of prosperity may define new levels of deprivation, it is feasible that it may not afford for provision at an *ideal* level. Our eyes can be opened to new ways of life without being able to afford it for all.
17 Oppenheim, *Poverty: The Facts*, p. 87.
18 A. Walker and C. Walker (eds.) *Britain Divided*, p. 141.
19 Ibid.
20 J. Waldron, 'Homelessness and the Issue of Freedom', 295–324.

21　Ibid.
22　Ibid. To increase regulation of public places seems a rather egregious example of brushing a problem under the carpet.
23　See Walker and Walker, *Britain Divided*, p. 142 and Oppenheim, *Poverty: The Facts*, p. 89.
24　Waldron, 'Homelessness and the Issue of Freedom', pp. 295–324.
25　Oppenheim, *Poverty: The Facts*, p. 88.
26　Ibid., p. 32.
27　Ibid., p. 29. 11,330,000 people (20 per cent of the population) were living *on or below* that level.
28　Ibid., p. 39.
29　Ibid., p. 46.
30　Walker, and Walker, *Britain Divided*, p. 20.
31　J. Mack and S. Lansley, 'Poor Britain', cited in Oppenheim, *Poverty: The Facts*, p. 9 and Walker and Walker, *Britain Divided*, p. 20.
32　Oppenheim, *Poverty: The Facts*, p. 10. We might want to add to this list of necessities, things like a minimum travel allowance for work and leisure and access to the media for citizenship, work and leisure, whether it be through public (libraries) or private (television and radio) provision.
33　Joseph Rowntree Foundation, *Social Policy Research Findings, No 31*, derived from J. Bradshaw et al, *Summary Budget Standards for Six Households*.
34　Oppenheim, *Poverty: The Facts*, p. 50.
35　Jones, *Poverty and the Human Condition*, p. 6. See also R.E. Goodin, *Protecting the Vulnerable*, p. 83.
36　Jones, *Poverty and the Human Condition*, p. 3. Jacobs, *Rights and Deprivation*, p. 67, similarly argues that it is important that we are able to act in a way consistent with our identity-conferring commitments.
37　Jones, *Poverty and the Human Condition*, p. 13.
38　Ibid., p. 11.
39　This is being increasingly realised by the British government. It is important here to conceptually separate private and public aesthetics. To a certain extent, we can affect the (private) aesthetics of our own homes. However, the aesthetics of our homes are in many ways bound up with and affected by the (public) aesthetics of the neighbourhood in which we live and which we cannot individually alter. This is important when considering the extent to which society is accountable for aesthetic deprivation.
40　J.L. Hochschild, 'The Politics of the Estranged Poor', 571. See also my discussion of reification in Chapter 2.
41　Jones, *Poverty and the Human Condition*, p. 9.
42　Goodin, *Protecting the Vulnerable*, p. 129.

## 2　Disability as social deprivation

1　J. Morris, *Pride Against Prejudice*, p. 17.
2　M. Söder, 'Prejudice or Ambivalence?', 227–41.
3　C. Barnes, *Disabled People in Britain and Discrimination*, p. 58.
4　Ibid., p. 96.
5　Ibid.
6　B. Massie, *Disabled People and Social Justice*, p. 29.
7　Barnes, *Disabled People in Britain and Discrimination*, p. 148.
8　Ibid., p. 180.
9　Ibid., p. 206.
10　Or at the very least in some cases, as we will come to see, non-inclusive architecture.

11 P. Wood, *International Classification of Impairments Disabilities and Handicaps*, Geneva: World Health Organisation, 1981, cited in Massie, *Disabled People and Social Justice*, p. 5.
12 Barnes, *Disabled People in Britain and Discrimination*, p. 24.
13 C. Barnes, *Disabled People in Britain and Discrimination*, p. 6.
14 Massie, *Disabled People and Social Justice*, p. 6.

### 3 Deprivation as a restriction of freedom

1 T. Hobbes, *Leviathan*, p. 261.
2 D. Miller (ed.), *Liberty*, p. 8.
3 T. Gray, *Freedom*, p. 22.
4 Ibid. However, Chapter 2 illustrated that many problems facing disabled people are indeed external, that is, they are social and environmental and are not secured by functional limitation. So, it should be possible to establish the unfreedom of socially induced disability using the traditional negative model of freedom, even though it is found wanting in other ways.
5 This is not to deny, as we will see, that effective legal freedoms can have some meaning. Suppose I was an old and uneducated black person in the American South. The end of legal segregation in university education might mean a lot to me, even if I were unable to study because, say, I was too old. Here, though, that the end of legal segregation might mean a lot to me would seem to be conditional on the expectation that others will indeed be *able* to study. Thus, while meaning can be derived from effective legal freedoms, freedom tends to mean a lot more if it is realisable, even if not to oneself at a particular point in time. I am very grateful to James Dwyer for this example.
6 J. Rawls, *A Theory of Justice*, p. 12.
7 Ibid., p. 137.
8 Ibid., p. 143.
9 Ibid., pp. 302–3.
10 Ibid., pp. 92–3.
11 B. Barry, *The Liberal Theory of Justice*, p. 56
12 W. Kymlicka, *Contemporary Political Philosophy*, p. 72.
13 T.W. Pogge, *Realizing Rawls*, p. 109.
14 Ibid., p. 114.
15 See, for example, J. Rawls, 'Social Unity and Primary Goods', pp. 168–9 and J. Rawls, 'Kantian Constructivism in Moral Theory', p. 546. Also cited in T.W. Pogge, *Realizing Rawls*, pp. 114–15.
16 T.W. Pogge, *Realizing Rawls*, pp. 114–15.
17 Ibid., p. 116.
18 Ibid., p. 115.
19 Ibid., pp. 183–4.
20 Ibid., p.184, footnote 28.
21 Rawls, *A Theory of Justice*, p. 73.
22 Pogge, *Realizing Rawls*, p. 178.
23 This question is addressed in Chapter 8 on Nozick and natural assets.
24 Pogge, *Realizing Rawls*, p. 164.
25 Ibid.
26 Ibid., p. 165.
27 T. Scanlon, 'Rawls' Theory of Justice', p. 181.
28 Rawls, *A Theory of Justice*, p. 204.
29 Ibid., pp. 204–5.
30 Pogge, *Realizing Rawls*, p. 128.
31 Ibid.

32  Ibid., p. 145.
33  Ibid., p. 130.
34  Ibid., p. 131.
35  Ibid., p. 132.
36  Rawls, *A Theory of Justice*, p. 61.
37  Ibid.
38  Pogge, *Realizing Rawls*, p. 133.
39  J. Rawls, 'The Basic Liberties and Their Priority', p. 44, cited in Pogge, *Realizing Rawls*, p. 136.
40  Rawls' assertion would not be true with regard to ideal theory if his conception of justice were to take natural primary goods more fully into account, for his difference principle does not attend to the fact that some need more resources to take the same advantage of their social primary goods as others. While this is an important criticism of his theory of justice, it is not a criticism internal to that theory, since he does not take account of natural primary goods in such a way. If he did, then so arguably would his difference principle. It is worth noting also that the idea being discussed, of incorporating a guaranteed minimum of means at one's disposal into the first principle of justice, could be adjusted so as to be sensitive to natural as well as social inequalities.
41  Pogge, *Realizing Rawls*, p. 136.
42  Rawls, *A Theory of Justice*, p. 246. See also Pogge, p. 136.
43  Pogge, *Realizing Rawls*, p. 139.
44  Ibid., p. 138.
45  Rawls, *A Theory of Justice*, p. 225.
46  J. Rawls, 'The Basic Liberties and Their Priority', p. 73. and Pogge, *Realizing Rawls*, p. 139.
47  J. Rawls, 'The Basic Liberties and Their Priority', p. 11.
48  Rawls, *A Theory of Justice*, p. 152.
49  Pogge, *Realizing Rawls*, p. 141.
50  Ibid., p. 140.
51  Ibid., pp. 141–2.
52  Ibid., p. 146.
53  Daniels makes a similar point when he argues that 'equality of basic liberty seems to be something merely formal, a hollow abstraction lacking real application, if it is not accompanied by equality in the ability to exercise liberty'. N. Daniels, 'Equal Liberty and Unequal Worth of Liberty', p. 279. Moreover, the fact that Rawls' first principle commands so much attention serves to reinforce the point that we generally take freedom to mean and entail something substantial.
54  See also, with respect to economic factors, N. Daniels, 'Equal Liberty and Unequal Worth of Liberty'.
55  Van Parijs similarly argues that 'Both a person's purchasing power and a person's genetic set up, for example, are directly relevant to a person's real freedom ... real freedom is not only a matter of having the right to do what one might want to do, but also a matter of having the means for doing it'. P. Van Parijs, *Real Freedom for All*, p. 4.
56  In a similar sense, Sen writes not about 'ability', but 'capability'. 'Capabilities ... are notions of freedom, in the positive sense: what real opportunities you have regarding the life you may lead.' A. Sen, *The Standard of Living*, p. 36.
57  This could be seen to go against Van Parijs' position. He writes that 'the class of desires that could therefore count as freedom-restricting according to the view of real freedom that is here being proposed does not include all desires that would be regarded as freedom-restricting if one of the "positive" conceptions of freedom had been adopted.' P. Van Parijs, *Real Freedom for All*, p. 24. An example of what is not included is a desire that diverges from some normative view about what a person

ought to desire. However, I do not think that such a desire should be ruled out as freedom-restricting at the point of definition. Rather, the idea that some desires might be freedom-restricting should be open to debate. Indeed, one might argue (while at the same time acknowledging the danger of such an argument) that some tendencies, for example towards paedophilia or religious extremism, are worth trying to liberate people from.

58 J. Feinberg, *Social Philosophy*, p. 13.

59 G. MacCallum, 'Negative and Positive Freedom', p. 102.

60 Gray, *Freedom*, p. 12.

61 This seems to be what Williams envisages when he writes that 'one has to put some constraints on the kinds of capability that are going to count in thinking about the relation between capability on the one hand and well-being or the standard of living on the other ... I think that it is difficult to avoid taking into account the notion of something like a basic capability ... we shall also have to bear in mind that we cannot simply take without correction the locally recognised capacities and incapacities, opportunities and lack of opportunities, because in some cases the question of what is recognised will be ideological ... We have to correct the local expectations of what count as relevant opportunities and lack of opportunities in the light of general social theory and general ethical criticism of these societies'. B. Williams, 'The Standard of Living: Interests and Capabilities', pp. 100–102.

62 The same might be said with regard to the stigmatisation of people who are more generally relatively deprived.

63 However pedantic or insensitive it might seem, it could be argued, for example, that the freedom of a person in a wheelchair to climb stairs is, in some cases, minimally worthwhile. That is to say, such a person might be able to drag themselves up the stairs with their bare hands. Such a conception of realisability could be said to be too minimal. We might argue, for example, that a condition of a freedom being called realisable should be that it is realisable without entailing physical pain or mental anguish. Then it could be maintained that the provision of wheelchairs and ramps or lifts was necessary to secure freedom, while the provision of turbocharged wheelchairs with whitewall tyres was not. The problem here is related to that of defining basic needs. Although much further thought is required, it similarly does not seem to be irresolvable.

## 4 The doing/allowing distinction

1 W.S. Quinn, 'Actions, Intentions and Consequences: The Doctrine of Doing and Allowing'.

2 Ibid., p. 294.

3 Ibid., p. 298.

4 Ibid., p. 300.

5 Ibid., p. 301.

6 Ibid., p. 305.

7 J. Glover, *Causing Death and Saving Lives*, p. 112.

## 5 Knowledge and intention

1 W.S. Quinn, 'Actions, Intentions and Consequences: The Doctrine of Double Effect', p. 334.

2 J. Bennett, 'Morality and Consequences', p. 97.

3 See J.L. Mackie, *Ethics*, p. 336.

4 B. Williams, *Making Sense of Humanity*, p. 57. The same criticism could be levelled at the distinction between intended and purely unintentional consequences, although I assume that the distinction is more obvious and so less descriptively malleable.

5 P. Foot, *Virtues and Vices*, p. 21.
6 Quinn, 'Actions, Intentions and Consequences', p. 339.
7 Foot, *Virtues and Vices*, p. 22.
8 Bennett, 'Morality and Consequences', pp. 107–8.
9 J. Glover, *Causing Death and Saving Lives*, p. 89.
10 Quinn, 'Actions, Intentions and Consequences', p. 342.
11 Foot, *Virtues and Vices*, p. 23.
12 S. Kagan, *The Limits of Morality*, p. 141.
13 Bennett, 'Morality and Consequences', p. 104.
14 Quinn, 'Actions, Intentions and Consequences', p. 343.
15 Bennett, 'Morality and Consequences', p. 104.
16 H.L.A. Hart, *Punishment and Responsibility*, pp. 121–2.
17 Finnis seems to be making a similar point when he writes: 'There are states of affairs which stand to some technique or technical process as side-effects, but which those who choose the technical process adopt as means (or even, sometimes, as end) and thus intend ... A secondary and in that sense "incidental" effect can be a fully intended effect; a secondary or supplementary means is still a means.' J. Finnis, 'Intention and Side-effects', pp. 41–3.
18 This is a departure from Bentham's distinction between 'oblique' and 'direct' intention, which implies, by the very nature of the words deployed, that 'oblique' intention is less morally reprehensible than 'direct' intention. I am arguing that there is nothing 'oblique' about the strategic bomber's intention and, indeed, that there is nothing 'oblique' about intention. The oblique/direct distinction suffers from the same shortfalls as the doctrine of double effect in that it places a moral emphasis on differences in the causal structures of harmful outcomes, mistaking them for differences in intention. See J. Bentham, *An Introduction to the Principles of Morals and Legislation*, chapter viii.
19 Bennett, 'Morality and Consequences', p. 107.
20 It may be more accurate to say that the death of the foetus in the case of removing the cancerous womb is an incidental or supplementary means. That is to say, the surgeon cannot save the mother's life without removing the foetus.
21 Hence my assertion that the strategic bomber must intend it 'the other way' if he bombs the factory when he is certain that it is full of civilians.
22 As was noted with regard to an intended second effect, there is likewise a sense in which a foreseen second effect, when it comes about, becomes a supplementary means by virtue of the fact that the end has not been reached without the second effect coming about. A foreseen second effect might thus be called a potential supplementary means.
23 Glover, *Causing Death and Saving Lives*, p. 90.
24 Hart, *Punishment and Responsibility*, p. 123.
25 Kagan, *The Limits of Morality*, p. 167.
26 Glover, *Causing Death and Saving Lives*, p. 200.
27 B. Williams, 'Ethics', in A.C. Grayling (ed.), *Philosophy*, p. 550.
28 J. McMahan, 'Killing, Letting Die, and Withdrawing Aid', 273–4.
29 Bennett, 'Morality and Consequences', p. 115 argues that the notion of intended as a means should not be entitled to a place in our basic moral thinking.
30 Williams, *Making Sense of Humanity*, p. 57.

## 6 Consequences, duties and rights

1 J.J.C. Smart and B. Williams, *Utilitarianism: For and Against*, p. 112.
2 The propensity for alternative sources of understanding, such as television images, to render more immediate situations of harm from which we should not remain detached is investigated in Part Three.

3 This is a large and complicated question that I cannot attempt to answer comprehensively here. Nevertheless, I think that the common-sense approximations that I make are fairly uncontroversial.
4 W. S. Quinn, 'Actions, Intentions and Consequences: The Doctrine of Doing and Allowing', p. 302. One might ask here whether such rights legitimate the doing of harm or whether they define what counts as harm. What Quinn calls legitimate harmful positive agency is not seen to be harmful in the same way as unjustified harmful positive agency. The capitalist might argue for instance that competition is economically beneficial and that the effects thereof can thus in no way be said to be harmful. It might also be contended that punishment is justified due to its beneficial consequences; it is not the legitimate doing of harm but the necessary protection of good by punishing the doing of harm. Whether these examples should be called instances of justified harm or instances of non-harm is an interesting question, although I do not think it particularly matters to my point about rights. What does matter is that we decide what counts as unjustified harm and that this is reflected in our rights and duties.
5 Quinn, 'Actions, Intentions and Consequences', p. 306.
6 Ibid., pp. 309–10.
7 S. Kagan, *The Limits of Morality*, pp. 117–18.

## 7 Applications

1 Part Three explores ways of augmenting the theory presented here, so as to ensure that we do not remain distanced from the hardships being described.
2 Again, consideration of what our reaction would be to the 'bizarre evolutionary twist' described in Chapter 2 illustrates what we might justifiably expect in this particular case.

## 8 Nozick's retort: natural assets and arbitrariness

1 J. Rawls, *A Theory of Justice*, p. 72.
2 Ibid., pp. 101–2.
3 M. Sandel, 'The Procedural Republic and the Unencumbered Self', p. 22.
4 R. Nozick, *Anarchy, State and Utopia*, p. 229.
5 Ibid., p. 226.
6 Ibid., p. 216.
7 Ibid., pp. 223, 232.
8 Capitalist rhetoric along these lines is discussed in Chapter 12.
9 Nozick, *Anarchy, State and Utopia*, pp. 225–6.
10 Ibid., p. 228.
11 J. Rawls, *Justice as Fairness: A Briefer Restatement*, 1989, p. 57.
12 Ibid., p. 56.
13 W. Kymlicka, *Contemporary Political Philosophy*, 1990, p. 82.
14 In addition, to argue that a snooker player's ability is natural could be said to be demeaning given the hours of daily practice that such players tend to endure. The same might be said with regard to other highly paid professions.
15 L. Brown (ed.), *The New Shorter Oxford English Dictionary*, 1993.
16 We might similarly question why some who are not naturally disadvantaged find themselves socially deprived due to circumstances over which they have little control. We could also ask why a nurse, for example, receives relatively small rewards in comparison with a surgeon, given that the surgeon cannot operate without the nurse. The inevitability of these dynamics can be denied.
17 Nozick, *Anarchy, State and Utopia*, p. 9.

## 9  An argument from democracy

1  T.F. Hoad (ed.), *The Concise Oxford Dictionary of English Etymology*.
2  A. Arblaster, *Democracy*, p. 9.
3  R.A. Dahl, *Democracy and its Critics*, p. 84.
4  C. Cohen, *Democracy*, p. 264.
5  W.N. Nelson, *On Justifying Democracy*, p. 129.
6  D. Miller, 'Deliberative Democracy and Social Choice', p. 57.
7  W.H. Riker, *Liberalism Against Populism*, p. 244.
8  J.R. Pennock, *Democratic Political Theory*, p. 159.
9  Nelson, *On Justifying Democracy*, p. 96.
10  Dahl, *Democracy and its Critics*, p. 89.
11  While negative vindications of democracy are often thought to be sufficient, it is interesting to note that different democratic procedures have little choice but to stress their congruence with underlying values when asserting their superiority. 'The democratic ideal is constantly being appealed to as a test for what is "really" democratic.' Pennock, *Democratic Political Theory*, p. 159.
12  Dahl's resulting optimism about freedom being extended through the practice of democracy only makes sense as a justification, as opposed to a vindication, if the promotion of such freedom is reflected in, or forms part of, the ideal of democracy.
13  S.I. Benn and R.S. Peters, *Social Principles and the Democratic State*, pp. 350–5.
14  Cohen, *Democracy*, p. 268.
15  D. Held, *Models of Democracy*, p. 270. Whether the self-government of different people can cohere so as to form a 'general will' is a separate question, although I assume that, for a 'general will' to be authentic, it is required that those who compose it are antecedently self-governing.
16  Cohen, *Democracy*, pp. 269–70.
17  Held, *Models of Democracy*, p. 227.
18  R. Harrison, *Democracy*, p. 163.
19  Arblaster, *Democracy*, p. 67.
20  Harrison, *Democracy*, p. 167.
21  'Consider, for example, promising, which is a means we have of moralising or controlling our social actions. Autonomy, thought of in the absolute sort of way, would forbid any such promises. For even though the promise is freely made, some of the will of the person making the promise has been handed over into the control of someone else. ... the will of the individuals is sometimes bound by something outside themselves ... the key notion is that of maximising, of there being more or less freedom, rather than freedom being taken as an absolute which is either possessed completely or not at all.' Harrison, *Democracy*, pp. 171–2.
22  Harrison, *Democracy*, p. 173.
23  Ibid.
24  Ibid., p. 228.
25  Dahl, *Democracy and its Critics*, p. 105.
26  Harrison, *Democracy*, p. 228.
27  Ibid., p. 229.
28  B. Barry, *Democracy and Power*, p. 57.
29  Cohen, *Democracy*, p. 274.
30  It could be argued that the justification of democracy discussed here does not cover cases where people have a permanent and profound mental impairment and thus lack autonomy. These are complex cases that raise issues that cannot be adequately addressed here. However, I think that the notion of respect can be broadened so as to ensure that the interests of all members of the community are protected. At the very least, those who lack autonomy deserve protection on the

basis of respect for those who care for and love them. For an argument along these lines, see, J. McMahan, 'Cognitive Disability, Misfortune, and Justice'.
31 Harrison, *Democracy*, p. 230.
32 T.W. Pogge, *Realizing Rawls*, p. 133.

## 10 Nietzsche's thought experiment: the idea of eternal recurrence

1 F. Nietzsche, *Thus Spoke Zarathustra*.
2 Ibid., III, 13.
3 Ibid.
4 Ibid.
5 A. Nehamas, *Nietzsche: Life as Literature*, p. 148.
6 M. Clark, *Nietzsche on Truth and Philosophy*, p. 262.
7 Nehamas, *Nietzsche: Life as Literature*, p. 149.
8 Nietzsche, *Thus Spoke Zarathustra*, III, 2.
9 Nehamas, *Nietzsche: Life as Literature*, p. 149.
10 Nietzsche, *Thus Spoke Zarathustra*, III, 2.
11 Clark, *Nietzsche on Truth and Philosophy*, p. 265.
12 F. Nietzsche, *The Will to Power*.
13 Ibid., 1066.
14 Nehamas, *Nietzsche: Life as Literature*, p. 144.
15 R. Schacht, *Nietzsche*, p. 264.
16 Ibid.
17 Clark, *Nietzsche on Truth and Philosophy*, p. 269.
18 F. Nietzsche, *The Gay Science*.
19 Ibid., 341.
20 Nehamas, *Nietzsche: Life as Literature*, p. 151.
21 Clark, *Nietzsche on Truth and Philosophy*, p. 269.
22 Ibid., p. 272.
23 W. Kaufman, *Nietzsche: Philosopher, Psychologist, Antichrist*, p. 281.
24 We might be able to do something about our lives, especially if we are young. Likewise, if we find the state of the world unpalatable given starvation, homelessness, deprivation, injustice and the like, we might be motivated to do something about it.
25 She might affirm the repetition of her illness in so far as it reunited her with her daughter. In addition, it is important to note that the example of Mrs Smith as it is used here is based on the assumption that her daughter is willing to renew their relationship. Without that assumption, it is more accurate to describe Mrs Smith's potential regret as being that she had not tried to contact her daughter and renew their relationship. Obviously, her daughter is free to welcome or shun Mrs Smith's overtures. If she shuns them, Mrs Smith might very well regret that fact but she cannot do anything about it without violating her daughter's freedom. In this sense, the alterable object of Mrs Smith's regret would be the failure to provide her daughter with the opportunities for a renewed relationship.
Extending this case, the subject of discussion is the regret we might feel if our society has failed to provide certain kinds of opportunities. Whether people take advantage of those opportunities is a different matter and, while we might regret that others waste their lives on one level, the liberal needs the conceptual space in which to affirm people's rights to waste their lives in so far as they do this without violating the rights of others. What is important is that they have the opportunity to do the opposite, that people's lives are not wasted through any lack of provision on our part. Thus, while we should not affirm the continuation of a society that deprives some of its members of important basic freedoms, we

cannot prescribe what people do with those freedoms once they are provided if we are to remain liberal. The provision of freedom necessarily entails the freedom to do *or not do z.*

26 While Nietzsche's emphasis here is on our own actions, this is especially true of things that people are subjected to that, to say the least, test the decency of even thinking in terms of eternal recurrence. For harrowing accounts of such things, see J.C.B. Glover, *Humanity: A Moral History Of The Twentieth Century.*

27 Clark, *Nietzsche on Truth and Philosophy*, p. 281.

28 Nietzsche, *The Will to Power*, 293.

29 Nehamas, *Nietzsche: Life as Literature*, p. 156.

30 Nietzsche, *Thus Spoke Zarathustra*, II, 20.

31 B. Detwiler, *Nietzsche and the Politics of Aristocratic Radicalism*, p. 193.

32 Nehamas, *Nietzsche: Life as Literature*, p. 166.

33 Nietzsche, *Thus Spoke Zarathustra*, III, 11.

34 Although such an idea may sound absurd in the context of Nietzsche's thought, his political theory can be interpreted in radically different ways. See, for example, B. Detwiler, *Nietzsche and the Politics of Aristocratic Radicalism*, and M. Warren, *Nietzsche and Political Thought.*

35 Clark, *Nietzsche on Truth and Philosophy*, p. 284.

36 Nietzsche, *Thus Spoke Zarathustra*, intro, 7.

## 11  The role of genealogy

1 R. Geuss, 'Nietzsche and Genealogy', 276.

2 F. Nietzsche, *On The Genealogy of Morals*, II, 13.

3 Geuss, 'Nietzsche and Genealogy', p. 276.

4 Nietzsche, *On The Genealogy of Morals*, II, 6.

5 F. Nietzsche, 'The Dawn of Day', cited in P. Rabinow (ed.), *The Foucault Reader*, p. 79.

6 A. Nehamas, *Nietzsche: Life as Literature*, p. 246.

7 See R. Havas, *Nietzsche's Genealogy*, p. 236, and A. MacIntyre, 'Genealogies and Subversions', p. 287.

8 B. Williams, 'Nietzsche's minimalist moral psychology', p. 76.

9 F. Nietzsche, *The Gay Science*, 345.

10 D.W. Conway, 'Genealogy and critical method', p. 329.

11 MacIntyre, 'Genealogies and Subversions', p. 290.

12 Nietzsche, *On The Genealogy of Morals*, II, 6.

13 Ibid.

14 Ibid., III, 15.

15 Ibid., III, 28.

16 Ibid., III, 15 and II, 16.

17 A. Nehamas, 'The genealogy of genealogy', p. 281.

18 Nietzsche, *On The Genealogy of Morals*, III, 15. Nietzsche might thereby be unsurprised at our failure to help in cases of social deprivation. He could attribute such a failure to a deep-seated, misguided and utterly unhelpful belief that those who are deprived in some way deserve to be.

19 Nietzsche, *On The Genealogy of Morals*, III, 20.

20 Conway, 'Genealogy and critical method', p. 327.

21 Nietzsche, *On The Genealogy of Morals*, II, 23.

22 Ibid., II, 22.

23 Ibid., III, 28.

24 Ibid.

25 Conway, 'Genealogy and critical method', p. 327.

26 F. Nietzsche, *Beyond Good and Evil*, 202. If Nietzsche is right here, his point serves to underline the need to animate reason; to use different sources of understanding with respect to cases of human hardship to make sure that we are spectating rather than ignoring. Then, by implication, we would be prompted to act, albeit in an appropriate non-repressive way.
27 Nietzsche, *Beyond Good and Evil*, 225.
28 Nietzsche, *The Gay Science*, 338.
29 Ibid.
30 Havas, *Nietzsche's Genealogy*, p. 221.
31 Ibid., pp. 21, 188, 222.
32 Nietzsche, *The Gay Science*, 338.
33 Ibid.
34 Havas, *Nietzsche's Genealogy*, p. 188.
35 Nehamas, 'The genealogy of genealogy', p. 281.
36 Nietzsche, *On The Genealogy of Morals*, III, 28
37 See A. MacIntyre, D.W. Conway and D.C. Hoy, 'Nietzsche, Hume and the Genealogical Method'.
38 Williams, 'Nietzsche's minimalist moral psychology', p. 66.
39 Nietzsche, *On The Genealogy of Morals*, I, 12
40 Ibid., II, 24.
41 Williams, 'Nietzsche's minimalist moral psychology', p. 76.
42 P. Berkowitz, *Nietzsche: The Ethics of an Immoralist*, pp. 73, 288.
43 Williams, 'Nietzsche's minimalist moral psychology', pp. 74–5.
44 Ibid., p. 76.

## 12  Other ways of seeing

1 J. Dewey, *Art as Experience*, p. 348.
2 R.A. Posner, *The Problematics of Moral and Legal Theory*, p. 40.
3 Ibid., p. 7.
4 Ibid. Posner makes a distinction between academic moralists and moral entrepreneurs. I consider that distinction to be unnecessarily restrictive and divisive. However, within that distinction, I am suggesting that academic moralists can benefit from employing more entrepreneurial tactics.
5 R. Rorty, *Contingency, Irony, and Solidarity*, p. xvi.
6 Ibid.
7 Ibid.
8 Posner, *Problematics* , p. 52.
9 Ibid., p. 34.
10 R. Rorty, 'Human Rights, Rationality, and Sentimentality', p. 133.
11 Posner argues, for example, that 'A successful practice does not require foundations.' (Posner, *Problematics*, p. 59). A lengthy investigation with regard to that claim cannot be undertaken here. Having said that, this project is based to a certain extent on the assumption that the way that we conduct ourselves and organise our society should be both founded on good reasoning and open to theoretical scrutiny. Whatever Posner and others think of that assumption, the use of theory is presently of practical importance with regard to discussion and facilitation of social change. One would not last long in a policy unit armed only with some photographs and a compact disc. What is being argued here is that an appeal to sentiment can augment that theory. Moreover, given that our current practices could be said to be far from successful, seeking better theoretical foundations for future initiatives could be said to be rather important. It is also far from obvious how we could constructively criticise or defend a particular practice without some sort of theoretical basis. For example, Posner mentions the

unprecedented criminal violence in America (p. 60) and we can assume that he believes it to be a bad thing. (By implication, it is a little conceited to claim that American liberal democracy is a successful practice, something that Posner can easily be taken to imply). If we pressed him as to why he believed it to be a bad thing, it is not at all clear how long he could continue to respond without mentioning something akin to the foundational values of liberal democracy.

12  The proliferation of television programmes such as 'Pet Rescue' and 'Animal ER' suggests that this is not as silly as it sounds. However, it is worth noting that the position here is not unsympathetic to the plight of animals, nor to arguments imploring that we treat them with more respect. Indeed, appeal to sentiment has been very effective in helping to eradicate the appalling cruelty bound up with, for example, fox-hunting. It is simply being suggested that reason is vital both to a sense of proportion and to the discovery of priorities in these cases. That said, there are compelling reasons to prioritise the provision of conditional basic freedoms and to use appeals to sentiment accordingly.

13  In present circumstances, people may very well be grateful for charitable hand-outs. It is not being argued that they should not or must not be grateful, but rather that they should not and must not be *expected* to be grateful.

14  In addition, the very possibility that a particular source could evoke different sentiments highlights both the importance of and need for background theory, to ensure that the sensitivity being unearthed is correctly channelled.

15  At the very least, saturation would render other sources less effective with regard to their propensity to augment or animate philosophical theory (unless there is something to be said for repeated and unrelenting exposure to sensitising sources). It is also interesting to note that, if appeals to sentiment were not grounded in reason, over-exposure would be much more threatening to moral progress. Grounding such appeals in good theory gives us a lot more to fall back on should people become unreceptive to them.

16  K. Joseph and J. Sumption, *Equality*, p. 74.

17  Ibid., p. 17.

18  Ibid., p. 125.

19  R. Boyson, *Down With the Poor: An Analysis of the Failure of the 'Welfare State' and a Plan to End Poverty*, p. 5.

20  Joseph and Sumption, *Equality*, p. 42.

21  Ibid., pp. 19 and 14.

22  Ibid., p. 78.

23  A. Haworth, *Anti-libertarianism*, p. 35.

24  The most compelling arguments supporting libertarianism are considered in Chapter 8. It must also be noted that being sympathetic to a libertarian position need not entail being at all sympathetic to many of the attitudes cited here.

25  Such tactics tend to go hand in hand with an emphasis on values such as thrift, the encouraging of 'enterprise' and applause for the charitable exploits of the better off. They could be said to have been especially successful during the Thatcher years, hence the phenomenon of the 'working class Tory'. Oscar Wilde provides an alternative view. He argues, for example, that to recommend thrift to the poor is like advising a man who is starving to eat less. See O. Wilde, 'The Soul of Man under Socialism'.

26  The short-sightedness of such a claim is expounded upon in Chapters 1 and 2.

27  G. Orwell, *The Road to Wigan Pier*, p. 130.

28  Ibid., p. 191. Rorty comments that Orwell wrote 'the kind of book which helps reduce further suffering and serves human liberty'. (Rorty, *Contingency, Irony, and Solidarity*, p. 146).

29  There are equally moving and harrowing descriptions of the experience of disability. See, for example, J. Morris, *Pride Against Prejudice*. I focus on homelessness

here because, Glen Hoddle (the former England football team manager) apart, homeless people tend generally to be subject to more, and more overt, slander.

30 G. Orwell, *Down and Out in Paris and London*, p. 205.
31 Ibid.
32 T. Wilkinson, *Down and Out*, p. 29.
33 J. Berger, *King: A Street Story*, p. 33.
34 Ibid., p. 36.
35 Wilkinson, *Down and Out*, p. 93.
36 Berger, *King: A Street Story*, p. 6.
37 Orwell, *Down and Out in Paris and London*, p. 206.
38 Wilkinson, *Down and Out*, p. 28.
39 Orwell, *Down and Out in Paris and London*, pp. 206–7.
40 Ibid., p. 36.
41 Wilkinson, *Down and Out*, p. 28.
42 Berger, *King: A Street Story*, pp. 106, 24.
43 Orwell, *Down and Out in Paris and London*, p. 207.
44 Wilkinson, *Down and Out*, p. 44.
45 Berger, *King: A Street Story*, p. 34.
46 Wilkinson, *Down and Out*, p. 78.
47 Ibid.
48 Haworth, *Anti-libertarianism*, p. 99.
49 Orwell, *The Road to Wigan Pier*, p. 76.
50 Ibid., p. 131.
51 Berger, *King: A Street Story*, p. 23.
52 Orwell, *The Road to Wigan Pier*, p. 71.
53 Wilkinson, *Down and Out*, p. 176.
54 R. Williams, *Orwell*, p. 126.

# Bibliography

Amundson, R., 'Disability, Handicap and the Environment', *Journal of Social Philosophy*, 1992, Vol. 23.

Arblaster, A., *Democracy*, Oxford: Oxford University Press, 1994.

Barnes, C., *Disabled People in Britain and Discrimination*, London: Hurst and Co, 1991.

Barry, B., *Democracy and Power*, Oxford: Clarendon Press, 1991.

——*The Liberal Theory of Justice*, Oxford: Clarendon Press, 1973.

Barton, L., 'The Struggle for Citizenship: The Case of Disabled People', *Disability, Handicap and Society*, 1993, Vol. 8.

Benn, S.I., and Peters, R.S., *Social Principles and the Democratic State*, London: George Allen and Unwin, 1963.

Benn, S.I., and Weinstein, W.L.,'Being Free to Act and Being a Free Man', *Mind*, 1971.

Bennett, J., 'Morality and Consequences', in S. McMurrin (ed.), *The Tanner Lectures on Human Values II*, Utah: University of Utah Press, 1981.

Bentham, J., *An Introduction to the Principles of Morals and Legislation*, London: Methuen, 1982.

Berger, J., *King: A Street Story*, London: Bloomsbury, 1999.

Berkowitz, P., *Nietzsche: The Ethics of an Immoralist*, Cambridge, MA: Harvard University Press, 1995.

Boyson, R., *Down With the Poor: An Analysis of the Failure of the 'Welfare State' and a Plan to End Poverty*, London: Churchill Press, 1971.

Bradshaw, J., Hicks, L. and Parker, H., *Summary Budget Standards for Six Households*, Heslington: Family Budget Unit, 1992.

Brisenden, S., 'Independent Living and the Medical Model of Disability', *Disability, Handicap and Society*, 1986, Vol 1.

Brown, L., (ed.), *The New Shorter Oxford English Dictionary*, Oxford: Oxford University Press, 1993.

Bynoe, I., Oliver, M. and Barnes, C., *Equal Rights for Disabled People: The Case for a New Law*, London: Institute for Public Policy Research, 1991.

Church of England, *Faith in the City: A Call for Action by Church and Nation: The Report of the Archbishop of Canterbury's Commission on Urban Priority Areas*, London: Church House, 1985.

Clark, M., *Nietzsche on Truth and Philosophy*, Cambridge: Cambridge University Press, 1990.

Cohen, C. *Democracy*, Athens GA: University of Georgia Press, 1971.

Cohen, G.A., *Self-Ownership: Delineating the Concept*, Private communication, July 1994.

——'Where the Action is: On the Site of Distributive Justice', *Philosophy and Public Affairs*, 1997.

Cole, P., 'Social Liberty and the Physically Disabled', *Journal of Applied Philosophy*, 1987, Vol. 4.

Conway, D.W., 'Genealogy and Critical Method', in Schacht, R. (ed.), *Nietzsche, Genealogy, Morality*, Berkeley: University of California Press, 1994.

Dahl, R.A., *Democracy and its Critics*, New Haven: Yale University Press, 1989.

Daniels, N., 'Equal Liberty and Unequal Worth of Liberty', in Daniels (ed.), *Reading Rawls*, Oxford: Blackwell, 1975.

Darwall, S., Gibbard, A., and Railton, P., 'Toward Fin de Siècle Ethics: Some Trends', *The Philosophical Review*, 1992, Vol. 101.

Dasgupta, P., *An Enquiry into Well-being and Destitution*, Oxford: Clarendon Press, 1993.

Detwiler, B., *Nietzsche and the Politics of Aristocratic Radicalism*, Chicago: University of Chicago Press, 1990.

Dewey, J., *Art as Experience*, New York: Capricorn Books, 1958.

Feinberg, J., *Rights, Justice and the Bounds of Liberty*, Oxford: Oxford University Press, 1977.

—— *Social Philosophy*, Englewood Cliffs: Prentice Hall, 1973.

Finklestein, V., *Attitudes and Disabled People*, New York: World Rehabilitation Fund, 1980.

Finnis, J., 'Intention and Side-effects', in Frey, R.G and Morris, C.W. (eds.), *Liability and Responsibility*, Cambridge: Cambridge University Press, 1991.

Foot, P., *Virtues and Vices*, Oxford: Basil Blackwell, 1978.

Geuss, R., 'Nietzsche and Genealogy', *European Journal of Philosophy*, 1994, Vol. 2.

Glover, J., *Causing Death and Saving Lives*, Harmondsworth: Penguin Books, 1977.

——*Humanity: A Moral History of the Twentieth Century*, London: Pimlico, 2001.

Goodin, R.E., *Protecting the Vulnerable*, Chicago: University of Chicago Press, 1985.

Gray, T, *Freedom*, London: Macmillan, 1991.

Grayling, A.C., (ed.), *Philosophy*, Oxford: Oxford University Press, 1995.

Harris, J., 'The Survival Lottery', *Philosophy*, 1975, Vol. 50.

Harrison, R., *Democracy*, London: Routledge, 1993.

Hart, H.L.A., *Punishment and Responsibility*, Oxford: Clarendon Press, 1968.

Hart, H.L.A., and Honore, A.M., *Causation in the Law*, Oxford: Oxford University Press, 1959.

Havas, R., *Nietzsche's Genealogy*, Ithaca: Cornell University Press, 1995.

Haworth, A., *Anti-libertarianism*, London: Routledge, 1994.

Held, D., *Models of Democracy*, Cambridge: Polity Press, 1987.

Hoad, T.F. (ed.), *The Concise Oxford Dictionary of English Etymology*, Oxford: Oxford University Press, 1986.

Hobbes, T., *Leviathan*, Harmondsworth: Penguin, 1985.

Hochschild, J.L., 'The Politics of the Estranged Poor', *Ethics*, 1991, Vol. 101.

Hyland, T., 'Disability and the Moral Point of View', *Disability, Handicap and Society*, 1987, Vol. 2.

Jacobs, L.A., *Rights and Deprivation*, Oxford: Clarendon Press, 1993.

Jones, J.D., *Poverty and the Human Condition: A Philosophical Enquiry*, New York: The Edwin Mellen Press, 1990.

Joseph, K., and Sumption, J., *Equality*, London: John Murray, 1979.
Joseph Rowntree Foundation, *Social Policy Research Findings*, No. 31, York, November 1992.
Kagan, S., *The Limits of Morality*, Oxford: Clarendon Press, 1989.
Kamm, F.M., 'Harming, Not Aiding and Positive Rights', *Philosophy and Public Affairs*, 1986.
Kaufman, W., *Nietzsche: Philosopher, Psychologist, Antichrist*, Princeton: Princeton University Press, 1950.
King, D.S., and Waldron, J., 'Citizenship, Social Citizenship and the Defence of Welfare Provision', *British Journal of Political Science*, 1988, Vol. 18.
Kymlicka, W., *Contemporary Political Philosophy*, Oxford: Clarendon Press, 1990.
MacCallum, G., 'Negative and Positive Freedom', in Miller, D. (ed.), *Liberty*, Oxford: Oxford University Press, 1991.
Mackie, J.L., *Ethics*, Harmondsworth: Penguin Books, 1977.
MacIntyre, A., 'Genealogies and Subversions' in Schacht, R. (ed.), *Nietzsche, Genealogy, Morality*, Berekely: University of California Press, 1994.
MacIntyre, A., Conway, D.W., and Hoy, D.C., 'Nietzsche, Hume and the Genealogical Method', in Schacht, R. (ed.), *Nietzsche, Genealogy, Morality*, Berkeley: University of California Press, 1994.
McMahan, J., 'Cognitive Disability, Misfortune, and Justice', *Philosophy and Public Affairs*, 1996, Vol. 25.
——'Killing, Letting Die, and Withdrawing Aid', *Ethics*, 1993, Vol. 103.
Massie, B., *Disabled People and Social Justice*, London: Institute for Public Policy Research, 1994.
Miller, D. (ed.), 'Deliberative Democracy and Social Choice', *Political Studies*, 1992, Vol. XL.
——*Liberty*, Oxford: Oxford University Press, 1991.
Morris, J., *Pride Against Prejudice*, London: The Women's Press, 1991.
Nehamas, A., 'The Genealogy of Genealogy', in Schacht, R. (ed.), *Nietzsche, Genealogy, Morality*, Berkeley: University of California Press, 1994.
——*Nietzsche: Life as Literature*, Cambridge, MA: Harvard University Press, 1985.
Nelson, W.N., *On Justifying Democracy*, London: Routledge and Kegan Paul, 1980.
Nietzsche, F., *Beyond Good and Evil*, translated by Hollingdale, R.J., Harmondsworth: Penguin, 1973.
——*The Gay Science*, translated by Kaufmann, W., New York: Vintage Books, 1974.
——*On The Genealogy of Morals*, translated by Kaufmann, W. and Hollingdale, R.J., New York: Vintage Books, 1989.
——*Thus Spoke Zarathustra*, translated by Hollingdale, R.J., Harmondsworth: Penguin, 1969.
——*The Will to Power*, translated by W. Kaufmann and R.J. Hollingdale, New York: Vintage Books, 1968.
Nozick, R., *Anarchy, State and Utopia*, Oxford: Blackwell, 1974.
Oppenheim, C., *Poverty: The Facts*, London: Child Poverty Action Group, 1993.
Orwell, G., *Down and Out in Paris and London*, Harmondsworth: Penguin, 1940.
——*The Road to Wigan Pier*, Harmondsworth: Penguin, 1962.
Parent, W.A., 'Freedom as the Non-restriction of Options', *Mind*, 1974, Vol. 83.
Pennock, J.R., *Democratic Political Theory*, Princeton: Princeton University Press, 1979.
Pogge, T.W, *Realizing Rawls*, Ithaca: Cornell University Press, 1989.

Posner, R.A., *The Problematics of Moral and Legal Theory*, Cambridge, MA: The Belknap Press of Harvard University Press, 1999.

Quinn, W.S., 'Actions, Intentions and Consequences: The Doctrine of Doing and Allowing', *Philosophical Review*, July 1989.

——'Actions, Intentions and Consequences: The Doctrine of Double Effect', *Philosophy and Public affairs*, 1989.

Rabinow, P. (ed.), *The Foucault Reader*, London: Penguin Books, 1984.

Rawls, J., 'The Basic Liberties and Their Priority', in McMurrin, S., (ed.), *The Tanner Lectures on Human Value*, 3, Utah: University of Utah Press, 1982.

——'Justice as Fairness: A Briefer Restatement', unpublished, Harvard University, 1989.

——'Kantian Constructivism in Moral Theory', *Journal of Philosophy*, 77, 1980.

——'Social Unity and Primary Goods', in Sen, A., and Williams, B., (eds.), *Utilitarianism and Beyond*, Cambridge: Cambridge University Press, 1982.

——*A Theory of Justice*, Oxford: Oxford University Press, 1974.

Riker, W.H., *Liberalism Against Populism*, Illinois: Waveland Press, 1988.

Rorty, R., *Contingency,Irony, and Solidarity*, Cambridge University Press, 1989.

——'Human Rights, Rationality, and Sentimentality', in Shute, S., and Hurley, S., (eds.), *On Human Rights*, New York: Harper Collins, 1993.

Ryan, A., *The Idea of Freedom*, Oxford: Oxford University Press, 1979.

Sandel, M., 'The Procedural Republic and the Unencumbered Self', in Avineri and de-Shalit (eds.), *Communitarianism and Individualism*, Oxford: Oxford University Press, 1992.

Scanlon, T., 'Rawls' Theory of Justice', in Daniels (ed.), *Reading Rawls*, Oxford: Blackwell, 1975.

Schacht, R., *Nietzsche*, London: Routledge and Kegan Paul, 1983.

——(ed.), *Nietzsche, Genealogy, Morality*, Berkeley: University of California Press, 1994.

Shakespeare, T., *Defining Disability: Conflict, Confusion or Compromise?*, Seminar delivered at the Social Policy Research Unit, York, December 1992.

Scott, J., *Poverty and Wealth: Citizenship, Deprivation and Privilege*. London: Longman, 1994.

Sen, A., *The Standard of Living*, Cambridge: Cambridge University Press, 1987.

Shaw, B., 'Poverty: Absolute or Relative?', *Journal of Applied Philosophy* Vol. 5, no. 1, 1988.

Singer, P., 'Famine, Affluence and Morality', *Philosophy and Public Affairs*, 1972.

Smart, J.J.C., and Williams, B., *Utilitarianism: For and Against*, Cambridge: Cambridge University Press, 1973.

Söder, M., 'Prejudice or Ambivalence?', *Disability, Handicap & Society*, 1990, Vol. 5.

Van Parijs, P., *Real Freedom for All*, Oxford: Clarendon Press, 1995.

Waldron, J., 'Homelessness and the Issue of Freedom', *UCLA Law Review* 39, 1991.

——'John Rawls and the Social Minimum', *Journal of Applied Philosophy*, 1986, Vol. 3.

Walker, A. and Walker, C. (eds.), *Britain Divided*, London: Child Poverty Action Group, 1997.

Warren, M., *Nietzsche and Political Thought*, Cambridge, MA: M.I.T Press, 1988.

Wilde, O., 'The Soul of Man under Socialism', in *The Complete Works of Oscar Wilde*, London: Magpie Books, 1992.

Wilkinson, T., *Down and Out*, London: Quartet Books, 1981.

154  *Bibliography*

Williams, B., *Making Sense of Humanity,* Cambridge: Cambridge University Press, 1995.
—— 'Nietzsche's minimalist moral psychology', in B. Williams, *Making Sense of Humanity*, Cambridge: Cambridge University Press, 1995.
——'The Standard of Living: Interests and Capabilities', in Sen, A., *The Standard of Living*, Cambridge: Cambridge University Press, 1987
Williams, R., *Orwell*, London: Fontana, 1984.

# Index

156   *Index*

Rawls's theory of justice 87, 88–89,
91, 95
disability: author's working model 27–
28; conventional view centred on
functional limitation 22–23;
dominance of sentiments in dealing
with 129; examples showing social
factors 24–25; need for accurate
definition 1, 19, 22, 24; official
definitions 26–28; as social
deprivation 1, 19, 25–26, 29;
socially induced 2, 27, 28, 29, 54,
79, 94; as tantamount to unfreedom
2, 46, 81
disabled people: inadequacy of welfare
measures for 21–22, 50, 79;
marginalisation of 104; physical
reality of functional limitation 19–20;
problems obtaining employment 21;
problems posed by mainstream
education 20
Disabled People's International (DPI) 27
disadvantage: disability as tantamount
to 26; functional limitation 93–94,
94; homelessness 14; natural/social
distinction 37–38, 43, 93–94; as
relative social deprivation 1, 17;
suffered by disabled people in UK
19, 22, 23
distribution 37; principles in Rawls's
theory 32–34, 88, 91
doctrine of double effect 3, 60–61;
effect on notion of intention 51–52,
59; examples of application of 61–
69
duties 3, 70, 73–74, 79; harm resulting
from neglect of 83–84; linked with
rights 74–75, 77; towards people who
are socially deprived 83
duty: Nietzsche on moralisation of 121,
125

education: as basic need 36, 104;
discrimination against disabled
people 20, 79; equality of
opportunity 37; and freedom 46, 49
employment 21, 47, 49
environment *see* physical environment
equality/equal rights: Rawls's theory of
justice 32, 33, 89, 95
equality of opportunity 36–37, 38
equality of respect for persons 4, 97,
102–4

eternal recurrence (Nietzsche's concept)
4, 107–17
evasion of responsibility 2, 79; denial of
intention as method of 3, 51–52, 58;
government's citing of lack of
intention 80; keeping distance from
hardship situations 82; in Nozick's
theory of entitlement 3–4, 87, 96;
recourse to doing/allowing
distinction 85; relevance of personal
commitments 72–73

failure to help 78; distinction with
harming 52, 53, 77–78, 86; intention/
foresight distinction 3, 59; rights
affecting moral appraisal of
instances of 74–75
failure to provide: moral evaluation 51,
52, 77, 78
Feinberg, J. 45–46
Finnis, J. 142n
Foot, P. 62, 76
foresight: distinction with intention 3,
59, 60–61, 65–66, 68, 79; and
harmful negative agency 55
freedom: democracy's potential to
provide 98–99, 100, 102, 104;
deprivation as a restriction on 2, 46;
distinction between legal/
hypothetical and realisable 2, 29, 44–
45; imposition of limitations on 53–
54, 81; MacCallum's definition 29,
46; postive and negative conceptions
45–46; Rawls's 'fundamental
liberties' 38–39; view of negative
liberty theorists 30–31, 96; *see also*
basic freedoms; unfreedom
free market economy: context of
Nozick's theory 91, 94–95, 96
functional limitation: in accurate
definition of disability 24; in
conventional views of disability 22–
23, 27; in experience of disabled
people 19–20; as impairment 25; as
natural disadvantage 93–94; and
social factors causing disadvantage
25, 25–26

genealogy of morality (Nietzsche) 4–5,
106, 118–25
Glover, Jonathan 57, 62–63, 67
Goodin, R.E. 16, 18
government: duty to provide for basic
freedoms 83; inadequate policies

Lightning Source UK Ltd.
Milton Keynes UK
UKOW03f0413230713

214204UK00002B/14/P